THE SK
K_ .

HOW I MADE BULIMIA PART OF THE PAST
FOREVER AND LEARNED TO LOVE MYSELF,
AND MY BODY ALL OVER AGAIN

By Anabelle D. Munro

~ Dedicated to people in the time before, during and after the painful ride that changes your life forever ~

THANK YOU to Huntly, Lily, Stirling, my parents and brother, Suzette Troché-Stapp, (the fantastic photographer and concept-designer of the cover photo, and years-worth of being my sounding board for this book), Glitterguru Productions, Natalia Dodd, Lauren Schoth, Olga, Nadine, Birgit, Cordula, Amy, Jan, Alex, Lureen, Bobby, Nazzi, Laurel, Harold, Matt, Ena, Milda, Harpreet, Erin M., Erin L., Dani, Marvin, Leanne, Jim, Christoph, Jennifer, Matt R., Ezequiel, Magie, Meghan, Reena, Ava, Monique, Nikki, Rogina, Brittaney, Daniel, Dilek, JoAnn, Marina, Susan, Senda, Ana L., Matt D., Agam, Christopher, Ange, Jacques, Georges, Debbie, Jimmy, Tracy, Chantal, Jason, Tilda, Jodi, Aimee, David, Kelly, Nicole, Ruben, Bill, and Del Weston.

◆◆◆

To understand how easy everything is, exactly that's the difficulty! - Anabelle D. Munro

CONTENTS

FOREWORD

Can one heal from eating disorders? No doubt. YES. And all the answers are within us.

Healing means to become the best judge and curator of who we are and what we are as a complex physical and emotional being.

Knowing what we need to be who we are, and following our bliss, equals happiness. Doctors, therapists, and medications are undoubtedly helpful as support in many areas during this process. Yet it is us who have to live daily life in our bodies within our personal and unique circumstances.

Because human beings are complex and multi-layered creatures, only a patchwork of symptoms is evident to the outside world. How can anyone else but us know whatever it is that we need to be satisfied? It is no one else but us ourselves, who can fully comprehend and navigate the unique set of challenges and environments we have to face. Therefore, it is also us who have to roll up our sleeves and do the work of providing what we need to feel fulfilled on all levels.

This effort includes not only our bodies but also our minds and souls. Becoming experts in being ourselves means that we have to watch our lives closely and in many different aspects. Especially in areas of unresolved pain, we have to check first. Untreated mental wounds and fears lead to a way of thinking that is preconditioned by outer circumstances. Being manipulated into action by unclear causes means that we lose control of our actions, without even knowing it. Often, as we try to find a band aid for a wound that needs way more significant repair, we tamper with our body-chemistry by introducing drugs, behaviors, or restrictions that force us to engage in compulsive behavior or thought that is toxic or self-harming.

When we look at eating disorders and addictions, these unwanted reactions (bulimia, binge eating, excessive drinking, drug abuse, etc.), or the unwanted inability to act (anorexia) turn us into self-destructive marionettes. Just like puppets, we are forced to behave a certain way, when the strings of our unresolved trauma, our triggers, are being pulled.

You might ask yourself, at this point, what the distinction between people who are suffering from eating disorders and addicts is. I lived through a variety of addictions and healed. This experience showed me that the boundaries between addictions and cognitive or behavioral illnesses are utterly unclear, and significant overlaps are undeniable. Therefore, you must know that I use the word "addict" liberally in this book and that it includes sufferers from eating disorders because of their shared behavioral patterns. Their compulsive and repetitive nature defines our unconscious reactions to triggers.

When something pushes our buttons, we are craving our fix, be it a tub of ice cream, drugs, alcohol, sex, or starving ourselves. I like to call these unconscious chain-reactions running our bodies like a computer program, the "autopilot."

These compulsive behaviors and reactions are in a way geared to help us survive, but if the pilot is unconscious and not able to get back in charge on an ongoing basis, due to depression, and/or addiction, the vehicle will crash sooner or later. The actual pilot, our naturally nurturing, kind, happy, and healthy self, must be awakened and allowed to steer his/her vessel towards making the best choices to be healthy again.

For an addict, the idea of being able to make healthy choices, sounds like a daunting set-up for an endless spiral of failure and regret. But what if there is a way to consciously put a stop to perceiving self-care to be a dreaded chore? What if instead, we allow it to be what it is: a natural, instinctual, fun, and relaxing way of being, as simple as breathing, taking a bath, or taking a nap? What if recovery is a fulfilling journey rather than a walk of pain and shame?

Addicts in recovery are often astounded by the phenomenal results that a few simple self-soothing rituals can add to their path towards healing. Choosing health, joy, love, and self-love is not only possible, but it is also our birthright. Reaching for wellness is accessible at all times, no matter how old we are, or how deeply trapped in years of practicing negative habits we are. Getting to know the mechanism of our human body and mind is the task at hand. Identifying and avoiding the gates that lead to self-imposed prisons that humans sometimes get stuck in, is the lesson. Learning to understand our inner guidance, given to us via our emotions, is the work that all of us, addicted or not, have to accomplish to live a free, conscious, and fulfilling life.

Based on the hundreds of addicts I have personally met, I noticed, that people prone to addictions are usually exceptionally kind, loving, caring, curious, and sensitive. Forming addictive habits can happen to followers as well as leaders. They affect the rich and the poor, the young and old, and claim victims across all genders and races.

You might be surprised - most of the addicts I have met have not only a keen interest, but also extraordinary abilities to live a deeply fulfilling life. I was amazed by this commonality because it is quite the opposite of what society perceives addicts to be. Why is that the case? Because when we see them at their worst, it looks as if addicts are acting selfishly and carelessly.

The predisposition for becoming an addict usually boils down to one word: trauma. If impressionable, sensitive individuals experience trauma, abuse, loss, or neglect, and there is no safe and sufficient guide close by to help them digest their traumatic experience, a heightened level of anxiety and the desire to avoid conflict and stressors are the results.

The process of finding coping mechanisms as a way to self-soothe via self-medicating the pain is hazardous when fueled by strong, suppressed feelings. If there is no understanding of this inner process and no knowledge about healthy self-soothing tools, and the person is in a toxic environment, an experiment can rapidly turn into a lethal trap.

Addicts carry a burden greater than they can manage. They don't know what to do with themselves. So over time, to not feel the helplessness and despair underneath, they try to escape and distract themselves from their wound.

An interesting fact about addicts is that they usually prefer to harm themselves instead of becoming psychopaths, who vent their inner rage about whatever happened to them. Psychopaths only feel relief when they make others suffer for them, while addicts tend to implode rather than explode. Their preferred choice is to rather destroy themselves than to lash out on others.

People struggling with addictions are usually empaths, people who feel other people's feelings, and who can naturally put themselves in other people's shoes. This emotional gift, when not recognized and used deliberately, can backfire, though. Not only does it make them extremely susceptible to what others think about them, it also leads empaths to defend and protect even their worst abusers. This hypersensitivity is why empaths are notorious for a lack of self-esteem. They blame themselves, before they blame others.

Opposed to what the incomprehensible and reckless behavior of addicts look like to the outside, they do care. They are genuinely stuck, knowing how their self-destructive behavior hurts not only them, but also the people who love them. This mind-trap, which makes them beat upon themselves even more, is the catch 22.

Let's remember: The original intention for trying out the addictive tool was to find a way to cope. The desperate use of the flawed crutch was to defeat pain and to help with keeping it together for the outside world. But instead of receiving relief, justice, and help, they have now stepped into the position of the wrong-doer. Their only answers to well-intended and desperate questions like "Please, why can't you just stop? Why do you want to destroy yourself?" are that they believe that they are stupid, horrible people who don't deserve any better.

Addicts are unfortunately consumed with guilt in regards to their wrong actions. These keep on piling, and piling up, and add only more destructive guilt to the confusing mess that comes with addiction.

The problem is that addicts believe they are doing all these horrible things that addiction forces sufferers to do. Constant feelings of utter overwhelmingness and helplessness, i.e., depression, is the result. In reality, it is the addiction, i.e., the coping-mechanism responding to the unresolved abuse and trauma, that controls them. The toxic habit "does them." Yet addicts blame themselves, as if they had a character defect. Looking into the mirror becomes an impossible task. A growing web of ever-increasing guilt and shame, hiding, lying, stealing, and pretending, entangles the addict in a life-threatening trap. Harming their bodies, minds, and social environments further are the self-punishment.

The belief to be "a bad person", is also the reason why addicts are trying to hide. They are ashamed and often in denial. They can't fathom that they have become their own worst nightmare, i.e., a defeated sorry-sight and societal problem when their addiction is in full swing. But here they are, trapped, embarrassed, exposed, debilitated, lonely, isolated, and powerless.

The longer the toxic habit, i.e., the symptoms resulting from untreated trauma continue, the more collateral damage accumulates over time. The thick outer layer of messy and confusing side effects and symptoms hide the root-cause, the trauma. And the addict is not even aware of it.

What can one do? The answer sounds easy but takes time and practice: one has to detangle oneself from every single sticky bit.

We need to open every self-imposed prison gate that we built by negative self-talk and blaming ourselves. Releasing our healthy self, waiting in there to be respected, heard, and loved is the goal. This self-love and self-respect can only come from the addicted individual him/herself to be effective. No one else can do this work, but every person for him or herself. A hyper-reactive, guilt-ridden and panicked, i.e., emotionally charged mind won't get the addict there. Neither will our inner "slave-driver", who is putting on the pressure. Only a calm, guilt-free, observant, and responsive attitude will - endless patience leads to the fastest results.

If people suffering from addiction want to feel whole again, they need to look at the complete, multi-layered person they are.

Most addicts are terrified by the thought of looking at themselves, because they get overwhelmed by the gigantic mountain of work that lies ahead. The adrenaline and cortisol levels are rising, and anxiety is creeping up. And what do you think the well-practiced pattern of addiction is pushing for right now: it urges the addict to escape from the stress ASAP. Stumbling into roadblocks when an addict is trying to clean up his/her act, is a classic trigger for relapsing into the habitual escape-pattern.

With the purpose to ease the load, this book wants to step in right there. The process of introspection is not as overwhelming as it seems, but actually quite simple. And there are hacks one needs to know.

If an addict manages to emotionally take a step back for a minute to leave the negative self-talk and judgment aside - including all past and future relapses - all addictions look quite similar. All of these toxic behaviors follow a specific structure, a so-called pattern. It's like a computer game maze, or better, a virus.

Since I have walked this path and have done the work, I can confidently tell you that now, because I was in one of these behavioral labyrinths, I see the "virus", the "pattern of addiction" everywhere I look. It is part of life.

We live in a world where it is almost impossible to escape the traps that get you stuck in one of them. Be it via media, medications, toxic relationships, drugs, alcohol, or food.

Our modern consumer culture has not only all the advantages but also dangerous side effects. Rule number one of advertising is to create needs that did not exist before. We live in a world that teaches us that we never have enough or are enough and especially that we are never good enough.

This kind of automated brainwashing and sensual overload bombards us constantly with thousands of directly targeted advertisements, suggesting the feeling that we need to have what we do not have. Emptiness, irritability, panic, stress, fatigue, burn out, mental and behavioral disorders like obsessions, anxiety, depression, and eating disorders, are direct results. In addition to our trauma, marketing, and PR, i.e., propaganda, manipulates us on a conscious and subliminal level.

I am way too sensitive and also too smart to not feel pain when I look at the problems, double standards, and unresolved questions in our world. I know I am not the only one who feels this way.

On the one hand, we live in abundance and waste, and on the other hand, addictions such as eating disorders have never been more widespread than they are today. I urge you to make the connection. Is it the individual who has decided to starve him/herself, or to overeat or stuff himself up to the brim only to get rid of everything right after just because of vanity? Really?

Anyone who has suffered from an eating disorder knows that this ugly disease has nothing in common with trying to be "pretty" anymore, once it has begun. It is the opposite: a disgusting, monstrous depression, fueled by self-loathing and guilt. Its grip is brutal.

Learning how to deal with this pit in the stomach when we notice how many reasons they are in this world to get mad quickly, precisely that is the main task and puzzle of life.

The answer lies within a sanctuary that only exists within ourselves and that we can access any time, no matter how ill, upset, or addicted we are. This place of unconditional love, wisdom, patience, forgiveness, and peace has no room for other people's negative input. Some people do not know about this inner realm, or they do not believe in it. They might have been overwhelmed or disappointed by life, by bad teachers, false friends, or fake gurus. Allowing this sanctuary to be left vacant or taken over by intrusive noise is the problem.

If our personal throne of power is not where we deliberately choose to sit, we cannot define a purpose for ourselves and feel unworthy of happiness. Finding this peaceful, serene place based on our truth is what the school of life wants to teach us.

Repeating patterns of the same roadblocks appearing like dead-end streets all around us challenge us to go deeper. But if we forget our unlimited potential to deliberately create and improve our reality, we allow other people's opinions, concerns, and fears to penetrate our lives until they eventually rule over us. And isn't it strange that we often seem to take especially the negative opinions of those to heart, whose advice we would never ask for in the first place?

After finding out where I lived the truths of others that didn't serve me, I had to learn, step by step, to wipe away all the confusing content that was smeared on my inner school of wisdom's blackboard. I started all over again. Back to 1st grade. Baby steps. And that's ok. It is better to start from scratch than to live a nightmare that keeps on sucking up my life energy until I turn into a zombie.

The process of going back to the drawing board re-wires our brain. This process is done best in an unemotional, curious, and practical way. Let's put on our inner lab coats and take "notes to self" in our imaginary notebooks. You will be amazed at how much power you have. It needs to be released. There is TRUE relief out there in this world: it is to be yourself and live your truth.

I opened the doors that once kept me from finding out who I am, and I walked through them. I revisited my past and handed out hugs, forgiveness, and kindness, where there had not been enough, which ultimately made me sick in the first place. My deep self-exploration turned out to be my skeleton key, my lock pick, a tool to legally open all doors that I need to walk through to be me. This multifunctional magic key is my self-realization and enables me to live freely.

It is incredibly empowering to have had this experience. Observing my body and mind, finding my unhealthy patterns, and overcoming my unhealthy behaviors turned out to be a gift. By studying our own personality, just like scientists would learn about any given topic or field, we can become real experts of our well-being, body, and soul. Knowledge creates awareness as well as mindfulness, resulting in inner peace, the antidote to anxiety, depression, and addiction. It gives us the freedom to make choices without being triggered into compulsive behaviors. Yes, this study takes time, effort, trials, and errors. But once we know what we need to be at peace, i.e., happy, i.e., healthy, and we make it our top priority to provide it for ourselves, eating disorders, or any other addictions lose their power.

Balancing between the desire to be healthy and the urge to give in to feeling overwhelmed is like dancing with a tiger. Initially, it is an adrenaline drenched endeavor because we must tame the wild thing first. We need to find its weaknesses, explore its personality, find out what it needs as a reward from us so that we can train it.

The day will come when the lever in the head moves to the other side, and it clicks. It is the moment when we boldly demand back our birthright to be the creator of our destiny. It is never too late to live self-conscious and self-determined again. Trauma can be cured. Self-esteem can be restored.

Also, innocence (contrary to general opinion) can be recovered. The human gift of forgetting, when used for our recovery, can wash away experiences that we thought would harm us forever. But before we let go of those painful memories, we have to look at them and overcome them with a forgiving hug.

14

I hated myself for so long, thinking that the things I did were the ugliest and most terrible crimes a person could do to themselves and others. Yet, the body is smart. It retains what it needs, and releases waste (both physically as well as psychologically), when we are in our equilibrium. However, if we choose to look away or even cover up our truths, we are sabotaging this kind of natural mental hygiene. We lose our naturally robust sense of identity, healthy sense of self, boundaries, and that honest self-esteem we so desperately need. Tending our wounds, if self-inflicted or caused by others, is a necessity.

A peculiar fact is that people may find that when they face their greatest fears, they might not be as scary or threatening as they thought, but rather trivial at times. Like, for example, when we give too much importance to what people say or think about us.

The most rewarding project of our life is to become our own best friend and best supporter. It is the only way toward clarity. Because even in this terrifying time of extreme suffering, addicts are beautiful, powerful, talented, and uniquely ingenious. It is just tricky to see and appreciate from the perspective of lack, illness, and worry. But darkness does not eliminate light - light removes darkness. To believe that addictive behavior disables our unique power and beauty is a thinking mistake that leads to more illness. Instead, while we are sick, we need to find a way to focus with all our might on whatever makes us feel good about ourselves.

The training of becoming an expert in being "Anabelle," is what did not only save my life; it also allowed me to appreciate the daily miracle of being alive again. It enabled me to reestablish joy, peace, pleasure, and gratitude as a mindset. Today, I feel like I once did as a happy, innocent child. Only better. I am an adult now - free and independent. "The Skeleton Keys," the book series, is the summary of my healing journey.

If you are currently suffering from an eating disorder or other addictions, I am thrilled that you are taking the time today to focus on your healing and personal well-being. This magical skeleton key (without the "poof" effect) that I found is the result of a 20-year investigation of myself, as well as a sociocultural, spiritual, nutritional, philosophical, and interpersonal journey. My formerly captive and tortured mind, soul, and body served as my loyal subjects during this extensive research project. I want to thank them for staying with me and guiding me safely through this dark tunnel. The "Skeleton Keys" journey stretches over a series of three books that build on each other.

Book 1, "The Skeleton Key," the part you are reading now, is my autobiographical part and describes important events and stages of my addiction from the very beginnings of my bulimia to the last relapse and a little beyond. But more importantly, it talks about how I experienced complete and happy healing. Reading this book is also a phase of your journey: The GOING INSIDE. The book invites, encourages, and guides you to become your "personal expert" through careful study of your life. Finding our sore spots so that we can nurse them back to health with unconditional love and forgiveness is the goal. Knowledge is known to be power, and the "devil" often hides in detail. I, therefore, tried to be explicit and detailed. I did not want to miss a piece that could help you to rethink and redesign your life just like I did.

Once you recognize your truth and identity again, despite the eating disorder, despite all the mistakes, all the shame, and suffering, you simply know where the path leads. And when that happens, and I mean that in a positive sense, there is no going back. Because once we heal from blindness, we have to close our eyes very consciously and firmly to not see.

Book 2, "Opening the Gates," is a comprehensive guide based on facts, personal conclusions, and practical advice that you would not find in a medical book. This volume also provides essential medical information. "Opening the Gates" is a guide to implement practical new approaches as well as the results of our conclusions in our lives.

When my eating disorder raged in me and for a long time afterward, I was relentless in trying to find out about all possible causes for addictions - especially eating disorders, of course. It bugged me that in a just, cause- and effect-based universe, people like myself, have to suffer from such a disgusting, hidden, and spurious form of addiction. I made finding answers to this nonsensical puzzle a big part of my life for many years. In volume 2, all my conclusions and insights stretching way beyond my personal life, found their home.

I discovered a vast amount of answers and want to share them with you, so you can understand the confusing mental jungle of this addiction much faster than I did. Following phase 1 of GOING INSIDE, the SELF-ANALYSIS in Book 1, phase 2 of the Book Series is the GOING OUT. In this phase, I invite you, to examine your external world, and your environments. Book 2 holds many suggestions for positive transitions and changes you can put into action right away and it gives practical advice.

Book 3, "Treat-Mend-Center," takes you on an extraordinary gonzo-journalistic journey that I have undertaken for you to explore and illuminate the world of therapy, the treatment center worlds, and medical help for addictions.

Phase 3 is about ACCEPTING AND NAVIGATING HELP. I never experienced any form of treatment myself, i.e., I did not consult doctors, therapists, nutritionists, family, or friends. Instead, I kept my eating disorder a complete secret. Because of that, I felt the unavoidable urge to explore the possibilities of professional therapy when I began to write this book series. That's why I have worked for you, my beloved readers, as your dedicated double agent for six months in well-known treatment centers in New York.

This third part of the book series offers a unique perspective on the process of medical/therapeutic healing. My observations at the eating disorder therapy centers are from an unbiased point of view. It solely focuses on the clients, their health, and what worked for them. But it also talks about what didn't work.

When I worked in the centers, I quickly realized that my secret research was a unique approach. Usually, we read about the insights of either a patient (or clients) or a medical professional, who has to deal with the treatment center as a for-profit business as well. People working in the treatment center industry are sometimes distracted from giving one hundred percent of their dedication to helping the client because of the pressures related to business.

Since neither money nor job security was of importance to me, I was able to focus on client issues from a perspective of staff AND former sufferer. I entered the world of treatment with sharpened senses so that my readers would gain first-hand client-focused knowledge, even if only based on a 6-month-snapshot. I intended to compile the best possible practical insights as well as give experience-based encouragement for this significant, positive, and courageous step. Readers who are considering to put themselves in the hands of a treatment facility or a therapist can use this book to find out what to expect. To my astonishment, I noticed that the process of trusting professional health-care and the industry behind it, especially in the United States of America, requires a particularly keen awareness of the complexities. However, the advice of being vigilant should not be confused with taking a pessimistic approach – on the contrary.

But besides being a thorough investigation, this book also contains a wealth of interviews, success stories, and a meal plan that was used at one center to stabilize the clients' diets. I saw its functionality with my own eyes as all nutritionists and clients used it at that treatment center successfully.

The "Skeleton Keys" series promotes the fact that a person with an eating disorder is not alone. Unlocking and transforming the destructive guilt complex associated with this disease is the book series' goal. It does not only speak about psychology, our body, and our society, but also about spirituality.

Living a healthy, happy life is a three-fold path where body, mind, and soul are in harmony with each other - I refer to this balance as the "equilibrium."

My spiritual development was an extremely relevant part of my healing, if not the most important one. I know that we all are made of light. Yours is as bright as mine and anyone else's. The only question is: do we hide it or let it shine?

Each one of us is exceptional, and nature uniquely expresses itself: no other person has my fingerprints, my face, my body, and my individuality. Unfortunately, we forget that when we grow up. We forget how incredible we are. And how unbelievably phenomenal it is to be on this planet in the first place - in this vast galaxy of waves, atoms, molecules, and space.

It is a miracle. Remember, the seed we came from and the one that hit the egg in the womb was one of a few hundred million (!). We were the fastest and most robust in this competition. What a crazy cell-dividing explosion of wonders started right after: our lives. Congratulations. But humans just tend to forget all that when we grow up. When we were little, however, we knew we were good. We innocently come into this world. Then, our experiences, and our reactions shape us, further or block us, heal us, or make us ill. The good news is that we can learn and grow if we apply our focus to it.

All we have to do is to sharpen our senses when we make decisions. To be at peace with oneself is an attitude, a mindset. And it is never too late to change course because we can even make a choice retroactively. When we change our perspective and opinions regarding past events, our present and future changes likewise and immediately. "Embracing our past," the process when our healed psychological wounds become our most valued teachers, is our magical super-power. I tried it, I lived through it, it works. I'm back to my old self, like the little girl I was before my bulimia. But with a few differences: I, as an adult, have way more choices now. I don't need any advocate to protect me anymore, because I have become my own best supporter.

Our rational self tends to make us believe that we have no choices in many ways, i.e., that we are powerless. But deep in our hearts, we know that the meaning of life is unrelated to being ruled by worries and painful experiences, such as eating disorders. If we manage to quiet our anxiety and let the dust settle, we all feel our inner guidance, nudging us towards who we are, and we know that we are always on the path.

THE SKELETON KEY

~ The Croissant and the Perfect Latte ~

I'm not a scientist, a doctor, a nurse, or a psychiatrist. Still, I'm a person who has gone through the horrible depths of an eating disorder for many ugly years. I've managed to overcome it - smarter and happier than ever.

I have found the key to my personal health, or better my WELL-BEING, as well as my freedom. I have rediscovered my natural, human innocence and experienced the miracle of complete healing from a severe and deadly disease: food addiction.

In my case, the dependency on a substance we need to live on, i.e., food, manifested itself as bulimia. Over many years, bulimia controlled both me and my social relationships like an unleashed monster living in my body. I suffered from a full-on, as in many-times-a-day-version of bulimia, which alternated with equally extreme periods of zero diets and overeating. Because of this, you will find that this book contains relevant inspiration and content for any form of eating disorder, not just bulimia. They rarely exist without the other "accomplices" showing up for some time. I want to share my story with you, so you know there's a way out, a complete recovery, a story of hope, and a second chance. If I could do it, you can do it too.

Eating disorders are very complex and challenging to understand. Because of that, they are often terribly misunderstood. It seems like people have to deal with them all their lives, once they are affected. This doomsday misconception stems from the fact that we MUST eat to live. Compared to cigarettes, heroin, or alcohol, where the abstinence of the substance is the key, we cannot just give up eating food. Eating and drinking are essential parts of life. We need food to survive. But beyond that, food is nourishment for body AND soul, and we should be able to enjoy it, not dread or fear it.

Even though eating disorders are a big problem for so many people, I have not met another person who has experienced what I did: a complete recovery from this severe illness without any therapeutic guidance or medication. I believe that there must be more, probably many, but maybe they move on with their lives without further ado.

For the last 16 + years, I have lived in three different countries, and in some of the most exciting international cities: Berlin, London, New York, and Los Angeles. I have a demanding, artistic job. I am an actress, director, producer, writer, author, and mother. The work in my area can be perplexing and heartbreaking. I love it, but I think you have to be sure that you want this extremely insecure lifestyle, and you also have to be a little crazy to start a career in the entertainment industry. At the end of this writing marathon, my husband and I have been married for 16 years plus, and we have the two cutest, kind, creative, healthy, and fun kids. Although some people might think I was lucky, I can assure you that there is no better or worse fate. As one of my best friends likes to quote, "The grass is always greener where you water it ..." What matters is the way we handle our life, i.e., our attitude. It is about how much love we put into things, including ourselves.

Thoughts like "but Annie and I are so different," or "if I have similar goals or more ambition or more self-esteem, more talent, more money, better friends, blabla... ", might come up. Should that be the case, I would like to encourage this person to re-direct the focus on his or her original intention to read this book. The habit of comparing oneself competitively and negatively while underestimating oneself hinders from being healthy because it is a part of the pattern of addiction. Nothing good can ever come from habitually thinking competitively, as well as negatively, about oneself or others. We are all at the same level. People, places, and circumstances do not matter in the end, especially if one does not consciously choose them. Losing oneself in blaming or self-pity is counter-productive and pointless.

You, dear reader, deserve the best, and if you haven't found a way to receive it in full just yet, be assured that it is out there waiting for you. Sure, what may fulfill me may not satisfy you, but we all know what it is like to cry out loud, to be angry, to laugh, to grieve, and to love. And all of this ultimately takes place only inside one's head, the stage of the drama of life. This drama may or may not include eating disorders, depending on the script or in other words, our inner dialogue that we choose - or not. Every life is different, and we stage our own plays ourselves. Let's take a look behind the scenes and unmask our inner players. I bet everyone knows them, the voices arguing in there about the "to-do-or-not-to-do."

I would like to remind you that everyone, addicted or not, has full creative freedom of choosing the end of their own story. It can be a tragedy but might just as well be a romantic comedy if we make the necessary changes. However, I know, during the time of its brutal and cruel regiment, bulimia feels like war, and humor, hope, and lightheartedness sound bizarre and far-fetched in this context. But if there is a way into this seemingly endless night, then there is a way back to freedom and peace. I promise it. By my own life. Should you personally be going through this right now, do not worry, we will get there, step by step.

Above all, I hope that everyone who reads this book, be it a sufferer, a relative, or friend of someone who struggles with eating disorders, and addiction, will find encouragement and the most in-depth understanding of your situation in my story. Should you be directly affected, I send you my utmost respect for the fact that you have found this book because it shows that you have already decided to use the tools that will help you to recover. There are people and paths towards healing around you right now: be it a friend, someone in your family, a therapist, books like this one, or all together. Reach out. Accept the help. I wish I would have had the courage to talk with someone about my secret back then - anyone - about that terrible black spiral downward, my fear and painful experiences. But I was too ashamed and too afraid to hurt and embarrass myself and my loved ones.

When I was in the middle of it, I thought bulimia would leave me in the state of a burnt, infertile wreck, should I be able to survive it. I certainly did not believe that I would ever find myself again in a happy, pure, simple, and so-called "normal" life. I thought I was doomed and self-destroyed, even if I would find a way to somehow not "do it anymore." As I tried to imagine my recovery, I feared that there would be only one ruined Annie left in the end. Someone, whose life would be like a burned-out battlefield of physical and mental left-overs after a long, all-consuming, lost war. Phew, sounds like hell and damnation. But that's not how it turned out to be. Not at all. I'm out of it. Done. It's over. With love.

Let's jump head-first into the harsh realities of my troubled past. I want to give you a real flavor of the fact that the stuff I am talking about is not based on theories.

When I think of those dark days, there is a particular scene that comes to my mind, a moment that has burned a picture in my consciousness forever: I walked along the cobbled main street of the small town in Germany where I grew up. These days I've binged and purged unbelievable masses of food many times a day. Nobody knew about it - nobody. With my inner eye, I can still see it as if it had just happened. The sun is shining so soothingly, promising springtime, smiling people all around - it's a perfect day. The street is full of lively, inviting restaurants, bistros, and cafés.

I pause for a while, and a woman comes to my attention. She is about 30 years old and sits alone at a table in one of the cafés, almost bathing in that white golden sun of early spring. In front of her is a large, beautiful latte macchiato in a glass. It's a perfect latte. The dark espresso is on the bottom of the glass, and the second third is the coffee mixed with milk. The last third is the most delicious creamy and perfect foam that crowns the cup with a fluffy, but not too airy cloud that looks like a smurf's hat, waiting to either be licked, spooned or sucked off.

24

I find myself staring at this woman sitting there with that delicious-looking cup of coffee. She is just as beautiful to look at and perfect. A sunbeam flashes at me, reflecting in her sunglasses, while the silvery light flatters her perfectly styled and slightly wavy hair and flawless skin. She is so elegant and slim. The scene could be from a French coffee commercial. The waitress comes back and puts down a plate with a croissant in front of her. The woman smiles and takes a spoon in her hand while she continues to enjoy the gentle warmth on her skin.

I still look at her as if spellbound. Bicycles and pedestrians are whizzing past me, contributing to the atmosphere of a perfect spring day in a better world that is just not for me. The lady licks the delicious-looking foam of her teaspoon and takes a bite. She smiles with her eyes closed into the light - a picture of bliss. I stood about twenty yards away across the street from the bakery, waiting for my mother to hand me freshly baked "binge-material," something she most certainly did not know.

Secretly watching the woman with the croissant and the perfect latte doing an ordinary and unexciting thing, I suddenly burst into tears. It happened so spontaneously and was so intense that I ran away to hide somewhere so nobody could see me - especially not my beloved mom.

Nobody should ever see me that way. I'll never forget what I thought "I'll never be like this woman, I wasted my life, I ruined it forever, I destroyed it all forever, my innocence, my honesty, my integrity, my happiness. I've mutilated myself, and I'll NEVER be able to turn this around ever again!" The thought processes that I have just described capture my mindset from these days. I love the example of the croissant as the kind of food that is "full of fat", "unnecessary" (this is how I used to call these types of treats) and mixed with full-fat milk from the "perfect" latte in the stomach, "contaminating" my body with "thousands of calories."

A croissant is also the worst type of binge-food ever, as it's hard to vomit. Puking coffee with milk is bitter and horrible, and a lonely croissant has no substance to it and will cause splashing. A croissant consists only of air and butter and turns into a tiny dough ball, once chewed and swallowed. My preferred vomit consistency was compact and soft. My way of relieving myself was first to stuff myself with sweet and quickly chewable food like ice cream or a whole cake, or two whole cakes. Or with a loaf (or two) of baguette smothered in chocolate hazelnut spread. The consistency had to be as airy and smooth as a soft dough, so it could effortlessly be brought up again. Therefore, water during the binge was important, too.

Gross, I know, but necessary to make you understand that I have been there. These are graphic descriptions here, but the purpose of this anecdote is to give you an insight into my life at the time, so you understand I was not just mildly dieting here and there. This illness had taken hold of me in a way where everything ordinary had turned into a bizarre, all-consuming abyss. How one thinks about food and classifies it when one has an eating disorder is cold, technical, and calculating. Just like any other advanced drug addiction turns into the dreaded business of getting the fix. There is no trace left of enjoyment - only the need to stuff this screaming hole in oneself.

But let's go back to the lonely croissant and the cup of Italian coffee. As mentioned above, this combination of food and drink was a terrible choice for a little puking session for many reasons. The small amount of food in my otherwise empty stomach just floats in a perfect (or imperfect) latte. What is much worse, is that it consists of nothing but pure butter, and the latte is made with whole milk (otherwise you get the foam is not right), a high-percentage fat liquid, which, unlike solid food, instantly "poisons" my system.

Why did I feel it was poison? Because the mind of a person with an eating disorder envisions fat like that. Particularly in liquid form. I was horrified by the thought of it entering my bloodstream almost immediately, only to be delivered straight to all my thirsty "arch-enemies": my body's fat cells. Everything would be already half-digested by the time I would order the check, pay, wait for change, and make it all the way home to my own safe bathroom. You probably ask yourself why was she not using the restrooms there, in the café? For me, that wouldn't have been a choice at all: no privacy. Purging outside my home was just too dangerous for me. The risk of getting caught by someone was too high. Trying to get rid of your stomach's content makes suspicious noises and is a smelly and messy endeavor.

A tiny croissant floating in coffee isn't exactly easy to control on its way into the toilet bowl. The only possibility to do it in the café would be to order more food to have a firmer, easier-to-handle spit substance instead of that bitter, bile-flavored, splashy fluid in my stomach. But that could make it just very obvious right there, that I have an eating disorder. What kind of young woman orders lots of food and eats it all by herself in a restaurant?

Also, it is way too expensive. Alone and in the privacy of my own home, equipped with a regular binge and purge supply, was the better option. How embarrassing this bulimia-autopilot felt. I despised myself and thought I was nothing but a thief, a liar, a pervert, and a loser - a nut job.

My brain speaks a very different language today. Sitting in a neighborhood café with a delicious latte and a pastry, like described above, is one of my favorite things to do. Today I do not have to worry about my figure anymore or about what I eat, even if I am not able to work out for a few days or sometimes even a few weeks. My body can adjust because I have learned to listen to it again, and I can intuitively rely on it to share its needs with me. I no longer use food as a tool to deal with stress. I have learned to separate my negative emotions from my eating habit (and no worries, I will describe in detail how I have achieved all this.)

There are only positive emotions when I eat, no matter what I eat: I enjoy food again without calorie counting or avoiding fat or carbs. There is no anxiety related to food and eating anymore.

Back then, I knew the calorie content of thousands of different foods, as well as their fat percentages. I stood 10-20 times a day on our scale to obsess about even the smallest fluctuations of my weight upwards or downwards. Today, I have not yet had a scale in the house for the last 20 years. I can feel my body again and listen to it and treat it with love and care. I trust my body, and I can rely on it to automatically guide me in the right direction by craving a healthy, balanced diet that even has room for treats like croissants. And because of this old memory, these taste especially good.

I promise by my own life, by my health and my body, that there is a way out. I mean, wholly and forever, and at peace with yourself and your living environment and food. And that full return to health and happiness is not to be confused with learning how to cope with the eating disorder in the sense of managing or controlling it.

Full recovery will not happen overnight, but it is one hundred percent possible. Once again, because it matters so much, the myth that once you have an eating disorder, you can never get rid of it, but can only find ways to keep it at bay, is not correct. The healing that I experienced is the opposite of being in a limbo state or having to worry about ever having to relapse again. What I mean with healing is to be free. The handcuffs are gone, and life equals joy. The last 20+ years of my life experience have been like that. I'm not saying that to brag, but to hold up a torch in the dark for all people who think that they are stuck in this nightmare for life.

There were no more slips in these 20+ years, and there will never be any again. Because it's over, done, part of the past. And all you need right now is the belief in the authenticity of my story.

Hope is a choice. It starts right here with your reaction to this first chapter: Do you dare to believe that someone genuinely learned to love food and herself again? And for me, cookies, chocolate, spaghetti, and birthday cakes are included on the menu and that with great pleasure. I considered all these types of foods once as bad, unnecessary, and unhealthy foods, and I would never have put them in my body. I thought of them as foods that I also would never be able to eat happily again in the future. Never.

I could understand that some readers might feel angry or unwilling to trust my story. Or maybe they doubt that this freedom can ever be part of their own story. That's why I want to let facts speak for themselves. I have only love for every reader and endless, sincere hope and knowledge that an ED (Eating Disorder) is 100 percent curable because I live that truth. I know that life is good and that well-being is natural. Therefore, our bodies, our brains, our hearts, and our souls have the full ability to get back on track and live a healthy and happy life. Our true self, our soul identity, is so much stronger than eating disorders, depression, anxiety, and all other behavioral problems. We must begin to understand the power of our thoughts and no longer see ourselves as victims, losers, or evil and damaged persons.

To honor ourselves in a way that a true war hero deserves is essential. It can save our lives. The rediscovery of unconditional self-love is the only real way out, leading to that new, happy, and healthy attitude towards life. An experience in which we appreciate our bodies unconditionally, as well as all the food that nature offers us. I hope that this book can shed light on rising above pain, versus giving up over and over again. All of us, as long as we live, can make the necessary changes. If we want to heal, two necessary attitudes are required, which contradict each other: letting go, without giving up.

We have to be ready to lovingly accept EVERY experience, including setbacks, disappointments, slip-ups, mistakes, and negative surprises. Still, we have to keep an eye on the big reward in the end, without wanting to grab it impatiently.

Now is your time to become the finder of your own inner power, the detective of your own life story.

Come with me, let us walk together through the shady streets of our inner cities and shed light on some critical situations that define the history of our eating disorders. I put my pants down in this book for you, beloved reader, and I hope that you will get the chance to smirk in between, too. Your innate sense of humor, even when things do not look so amusing, is the voice you should always listen to unless it is self-deprecating and sarcastic.

I know - eating disorders are the most lethal mental illness of all and not at all a laughing matter. But being able to laugh about oneself and the bizarre situations that one has to deal with on this rough planet, is a tell-tale sign of victory over our triggers and oppressors - it gives us back our power.

Welcome to this HUGE THINK TANK, into which we will immerse ourselves. It will be an intense experience to recognize and resolve blockages and misunderstandings on the way.

I hope you are going on an epic journey. With you as the hero in your own story - just as I had to become the heroine in mine. Let my odyssey into the depths of my eating disorder's origins and back serve as your research framework for your epiphanies. I hope there will be MANY. As I do NOT have all the answers regarding your personal journey, I have the most important piece of information related to it: YOU HAVE ALL THE ANSWERS.

So, let's go ahead and kick some ED-butt.

THIS KID IS A WEIRDO

~ Family, Food, and Faith Habits ~

As you might now know from the croissant story, I was born in a little town in Germany, a small but very picturesque, and cultured place.

The day I emerged from my wonderful mother's womb was a Sunday in spring. The blossoms were about to explode, eager to show off their vibrant colors to attract the bees and butterflies.

My mother told me that my arrival had started with quite some drama. Both of my feet came out looking crooked, and all my mother could think of was, "Oh no, a girl and no ballet." A few days of massage would, however, fix the issue, and my feet came out flawless and ready to walk many steps. My mother remembers the time at the hospital with me as very special. She told me that she sensed a heightened level of sensitivity to sounds and light within me. According to mum's story of my first few hours, there was a bird singing in the tree outside the hospital window. She looked in my barely opened eyes and noticed how intensely I was listening, with my already then apparent "thinking-frown" on my forehead, as if I was trying to decode the language of the birds. That frown would never leave me.

I would say my eating disorder had its first contribution from society right there and then, lying in the arms of my loving mum with my scrunched-up forehead.

When I was born, it used to be the general consent of Western medicine that nursing a child with breastmilk was something close to a crime. People at the time believed that it was a way safer option to bottle-feed with formula, where one could accurately measure and monitor how much of each nutrient would enter the baby's system.

Being a mother myself, who has nursed both of her children for 21 months, I can only say that I am truly saddened about the fact that my mother and I lost out on this bonding experience due to not knowing it better. My mum belonged to a generation that still believed anything that a doctor would say; she recalls a nurse on duty that told her that "she didn't even have enough milk for a cup of coffee, even if she wanted to breastfeed." That was that.

When I went to a breastfeeding class for my first baby many years later, it dawned on me: those few drops that had been mockingly described to my mum as "not being enough" had been the sacred drops of colostrum, the highly nutritious milk for the new-born! The new mother's breasts produce this potent first milk only for a few days until the actual breastmilk comes in.

Beyond the nutritional value and the long-term protection from allergies, diseases, and ADDICTIONS, my mum and I would lose out much more than that, as I know from my own experience with my kids. The emotional rebound place, where the most deep-seated attachment between mother and child flourishes, was something my mum and I would not experience at the early stages. Sure, we love each other, and she is a very tender, creative, and loving mum, but I know the difference now, having kids myself.

I firmly believe that for me, the lack of that experience as a baby resulted in me developing a thin skin. Skin-rashes, nervous nail-biting and anxiety, can very likely be directly linked to it. I'm by the way not upset about all this but glad instead to know these facts. It is this kind of clue that we are looking for to become experts in being ourselves. SELF-ADVOCATES.

My evidence here tells me that I need to protect my skin and immune system just a tad more than the average person. I also need to keep an eye on my anxieties. Because I am aware of them now, I can identify and name these feelings now instead of just feeling mysteriously "unwell." I can keep an eye on early warning signs. This way, I can counteract them right away with self-soothing tools that I learned over the years. More about that in detail later, let's go back to my childhood.

Both of my parents are teachers, and I have an older brother. The four of us lived in a lovely grand old house: my granny, aunt, and two cousins resided in the apartment above us. It was a good set up and idyllic, but there was also conflict between the two families. In this seemingly cozy nest, housing our large family, my aunt had just gotten divorced from her husband because of his alcoholism and the domestic violence related to it. My mum and auntie also had grown up without a dad. Their father, the Opa that I never met, had died in WWII. Sadly, a constant battle of comparison and jealousy between the families was the unfortunate coping tool that was used to deal with this family trauma.

I would always find myself being caught in the middle, trying desperately to make the other party understand that everyone was right and lovable, even if troubled. It was a lost cause. But there was also a lot of love.

My primary caregiver during my early childhood was my grandma Mimi. God knows how Grandma Mimi, being in her 70s, coped with running after little toddlers, while she was taking care of two households - my mum's and my aunt's upstairs. Again, seeing my childhood with my mum-eyes today makes me wonder how Mimi kept us busy. Did she put us in front of the TV? I most certainly do not recall any kind of reading time or going out to the park with her. She was way too busy with making the beds, cooking, and other work in the house. My mother doesn't remember either what my Oma did with us all day, but my inclination to TV addiction is maybe related to how we have spent our first three years before going to preschool. God only knows, and Oma Mimi, bless her heart. She was a kind, sweet, and caring dear-heart and indeed did her best.

When it came to food, I remember refusing to eat many dishes, and these memories go back to when I was at the age of three. I, for example, felt repulsed by raw mushrooms, raw tomatoes, and meat. However, I could eat mushrooms or tomato if they were canned. The meat was only edible at all when it was a finely minced sausage like salami or, to the amusement of my parents, expensive pate. But even in these salty, finely minced variations of meats, there was a particular flavor in it that simply disgusted me. I can only describe this flavor as "the taste of death." Cadaver. Besides this "special flavor," the other thing about meat that repulsed me most was when it had fatty veins and gristle in it. Not because it was making me fat, I didn't know and care about that when I was little. I was grossed out by the disgusting sensations in my mouth caused by this un-chewable rubber-like goo that would not go down forever. Thinking about eating the remains of something that I would prefer to stroke or cuddle than put in my tummy made me sick. God knows why, because everyone else in my family is a passionate carnivore.

As a result of being the odd one out, I just thought about myself as being a bit abnormal. I didn't have a choice when it came to eating meat anyway. It was served every day. If a bite had that specific cadaver texture or flavor, I would try all the tricks in the book like drenching and drowning it in sauce or lemon juice. When I succeeded, i.e., when I managed to swallow the darn piece after 300 chews, I felt pleased with myself that I was a good eater. But most of the time, I got pale and had to spit it out, unable to finish my plate because my stomach was upset.

On special occasions, my family and I would go to a Greek Restaurant in the countryside. They had an open wood grill, and I loved the smell there. My brother and I always had the schnitzel. It came with that delicious gravy, the best French fries, and even their ketchup was the best in the world if there is such a thing.

I loved this schnitzel because it was almost paper-thin. The breading and the gravy were the primary flavors on this plate. But even if the meat was hammered flat like a flounder, sometimes it still had a vein of fat in it. A disgusting, un-chewable piece, right there in my mouth.

As usual, I went pale, stopped chewing, and ran to the bathrooms to spit it out. Reading this back to myself, I notice that I must have had some sort of anxiety attack when that happened.

There, in the restroom, I would stay locked into the cubicle for about twenty minutes to avoid having to finish my plate. For me, the whole meal was now contaminated. Just looking at it made me gag. But there was another reason for hiding in the bathroom for such a long time: embarrassment. I just couldn't handle the thought of giving back the full plate. I didn't want to come across as the spoiled brat.

On top of the disappointment I would see in my parent's eyes, the waiters would always make jokes about me. Or they pretended to be sad when they cleared the table, and I did not want to look into their faces.

Back then, in the small bathroom with the beige brown tiles and the strong, uber artificial lemon odor, I would sit, cry a bit, and wondered why I was so cuckoo. After I was sure that the rest of my family had finished their meals, and that the waiter had taken away the plates, I prepared myself mentally for my walk-of-shame back to my seat.

My parents and my brother most certainly didn't understand why I would always run off as if a tarantula had sat on my plate and would only roll their eyes at me. Anabelle had done her little "weird" thing again. I felt ashamed of myself. I was only seven years old, with no diet intention - only the natural instinctive disgust when it came to certain foods and an unhealthy dose of shame for being ungrateful and weird.

Another clue! Little did I know back then that most kids are food weirdos and that they have individual preferences or types of food they just won't eat. My parents didn't have that information either. Not about the strange behavior kids can exhibit when it comes to food, not regarding how parents can help children to overcome their anxieties and also not regarding nutrition and if it is detrimental to include meat into a child's diet, or not. We are talking times way before the internet, cell phones, and social media.

Parents of the way more connected digital generation, can share their concerns and stories much better than it was possible in those days. Today it is common knowledge that a child's growing body is susceptible and that the communication between the belly and the brain is still very much intact.

Small children are not shy to express the messages their bodies are sending to them: they cry, shout, and even spit back in their mommies' faces, what they don't like. Our young bodies develop fast and quickly adapt from drinking milk to eating easily digestible baby food to eating all other foods. A few raw foods like mushrooms, which I couldn't eat when I was young, can indeed contain toxic substances.

Little kids know what is right for them when it comes to natural, unprocessed food. But please, do not confuse this statement with letting kids have their way with candy. I am talking about healthy food choices. If my parents could have encouraged me to eat an adequate substitute instead of forcing me to eat what THEY consider normal food, I would not have been disturbed in my natural relation to food so early on. I would have been quite okay.

Was there anything you didn't want to eat but had to? Do you remember the times you suppressed your instincts in terms of food so that you would fit in? Or were you left to your own devices and had all access to unhealthy foods, instead?

My parents, as mentioned above, didn't know too much about the innate wisdom of children when it came to food choices. I remember that my dad told me that my fingernails and teeth would fall out if I wouldn't eat meat. Trust me, this horror vision scared me so much that I broke out in tears. It surely made me continue to try at least my hardest when it came to eating meat, even IF there was some gristle in it. Out of fear, I retrained myself over and over to like it.

I do not hold grudges against my dad, not at all. He just tried to be a good father and was indeed worried that I would miss out on vital minerals and protein.

I am not against eating meat, either. I am not AGAINST anything in general. One of the many lessons learned through my recovery and healing is that I am only FOR things anymore. Anything can be a poison or a cure, depending on the amount. In fact, I feel great appreciation for all the meat that I have consumed in my life, too. When I was making the first significant progress with my bulimia recovery, I felt that I needed to eat a lot of red meat and chicken. My body was very much out of balance and malnourished. I had found out that obsessing over what to eat and what not to, was part of my problem and at the time, meat was way more easily accessible everywhere than meat alternatives. It was a readily available source of protein that I could cook without having to over-think my meal-planning for too long.

Back then, vegetarians needed to spend some extra thought on getting proteins and fatty acids via nuts, beans, and a small choice of soy products to fulfill their bodily needs. Vegetarian protein products were also pricey and only available in specialized health food stores. I truly owe all the cows, chicken, and fish my utmost gratitude for having given their lives to make mine less complicated in a difficult time.

It is incredibly insightful to bring your food history into a context with your parents eating habits and that you go way back when to dig for information. We need to find as many auto-pilot-programs and pre-sets as possible and reevaluate them into two categories:

> 1: Is this auto-pilot helping me to be happy and at peace with myself and the world today?

> Or

> 2: Is this auto-pilot destructive, i.e., toxic, harmful, based on other people's opinion, inauthentic, hazardous, etc. in any way?

Since we are now old enough to figure out which one is which, we can simply keep the best and choose to get rid of the bad ones. We are free to let unhealthy programs, habits, and beliefs go at any time, even if mama told us that "the sun wouldn't shine the next day" if we don't eat all our peas.

The earlier these pre-sets, i.e., habits are formed, the more powerful they can be. Still, they are not more complicated to remove than the others, once you detect them. New habits might take a bit longer to practice, that's all. To FIND them is the artistry.

Right now, I want to invite you to examine the regional diet you grew up with, paired with home-cooked dinner memories. All these learned ideas about food and eating shape our eating habits. The relation to our family members and food as a part of sharing life is a twisted dance.

On the one hand, certain foods evoke warm memories of our family, and they remind us of belonging somewhere and having a home until this very day. Depending on the kind of food, this primal, emotional connection can be a subconscious reason for comfort eating – we must observe if we sometimes crave certain foods because we want to connect with our roots.

On the other hand, you might feel upset about the fact that you didn't get much of a choice when it comes to negative food habits that were practiced in your family, like watching TV during dinner, only eating take-out, access to too much candy, and juice-overload, etc.

Whatever you may discover, I strongly recommend staying away from pointing fingers, neither towards yourself or anyone else. Blaming won't be an effective method to release those patterns and only gets one half-way and forever not there, where one wants to be. Forgiveness and implementing change from a peaceful standpoint, is what we want, instead.

Early childhood food habits do not only condition us in regards to what we eat but also how we eat and how we feel when we eat, as in either grateful and satisfied or ashamed and guilty. In my family, for example, it was considered good manners to always finish what was on the plate. Our parents and grandparents didn't implement this rule because they were mean, though - leaving food on your plate was considered wasteful. This is just the way it was. Even if that meant many times that I would eat much more than I wanted or needed, or else I felt terribly guilty (like in the Greek restaurant). This form of food etiquette was most certainly not intended by anyone to make me develop an eating disorder. But it contributed.

No matter how much pressure or sometimes even carelessness and neglect we experienced from our primary caretakers. Most of the time, they probably didn't know any better. They have learned those from their parents and their parents from theirs, and so on.

When I was little and felt like the weirdo in my family, I had not yet found my spot, my own identity within our unit. We all need to define this spot for ourselves. The path of my recovery forced me to figure it out. Part of this journey was the need to get to know my family very well, way beyond the infallible, perfect, and all-knowing higher power that I made them out to be as a kid.

By trying to put myself in my ancestor's shoes, I slowly developed an understanding of why some of their teachings were so off. This understanding helped me not only to forgive but also to clarify my own thoughts and conclusions about the matters of this world. I could, so to say, wholeheartedly update their theories and create my own truths. Studying my folks took time and conscious effort. Do you know your parents and how they were brought up? I encourage you to find out as much as you can about them. There is so much to ask and discover. More clues! More pieces for your personal skeleton key to unlock every closed door in life!

In terms of my family's food- and eating history, I took a closer look at the fact that both of my parents grew up as war children. They were born in 1939 and 1943, at the end of World War II in Germany. Food was something that one stored in one's body asap if there was any. Times were very different in Germany; babies died because there wasn't enough to eat. People like my grandfather, who died in Russia as a prisoner of war, ate rats and drank out of dirty rain-pits.

Then, later on, my parents were blessed with the food luxuries of a Post-Wirtschafts-Wunder-Germany (the economic miracle that happened in the '50s) and the matching healthy appetite to gobble it up, born out of deprivation. My parents need their sausages, hams, and cheeses in their stuffed fridge, to feel whole and safe. That, of course, influenced my eating habits.

I grew up eating many foods in an inappropriate measure, without even wanting to eat at times. The rule of always having to finish my plate with the help of implementing guilt and shame was a potent one. The result of these not quite perfect eating habits was a slight potbelly that I felt self-conscious about as early as I can remember.

Alas, it would take me 20 years to let go of my feelings of guilt towards the fact that my granddad starved, and that children in Africa have to die because they have not enough to eat, while we throw our food away or, as in my case, we throw it up. In my recovered adulthood, not finishing my plate anymore when I'm too full was a significant accomplishment for me for the following reasons: firstly, overcoming guilt, and secondly, retraining my stretched stomach muscles that seemed to belong to an elephant, thanks to bulimia. Getting my stomach back to average size, and re-developing a communication with my body that tells me when I am fully satisfied, took trust and time.

I DO NOT CHOOSE TO FEEL GUILTY ANYMORE. I can't carry the guilt of the world on my shoulders. I can't be sick anymore, because I need my strength and health.

Details are potent because we like to trivialize or overlook them. As mentioned in the introduction, the devil is in the detail. Specific rules that were given to you by others like "you have to eat meat to be healthy," or "you have to finish your plate" were contributing factors for me. They seemed so small and implemented since ever - they were almost invisible. These blindly accepted inner mantras, these little one-liners that are stuck in our mental membrane, makes us sick.

These seemingly small grains of sand disrupt our engine and make us believe that the problem, i.e., the breakdown, is enormous and impossible to solve. But in fact, it often consists of a sum of minuscule issues that we CAN address, one by one. If only we could detect them in the chaos they cause! Especially when it comes to our core belief-system, the power of invisible, blindly adapted ideas, is mighty. Examples of such so-called "wisdoms" are: "Life is just not fair," "Life is hard," "Love hurts," "You can never heal from an eating disorder, you can only learn to manage it," etc.

I like to call these almost invisible disruptors of our belief-system, these collected garbage-"wisdoms," "shitsdoms." They are nothing but toxic one-liners that make us feel bad or sick - never better.

Born out of the guilting and shaming methods that the older generations still used to educate kids, especially in Germany, where a guilt-complex is cultural heritage, almost everything embarrassed me. "What would others think?" was a standard line that was used to reign children and adults back in, when they didn't behave according to the rules. I was that thin-skinned child that took this question way too much to heart.

Often, our emotional and purely physical triggers, such as allergies or natural aversions, are all mixed up. But diligence pays off. What these observations taught me about myself, was that I had to throw up quite a lot, without sticking my finger down my throat, a long time before bulimia became a coping mechanism for me. There are more examples than the thought of meat: it made me for example sick, when there was the slightest risk of exchanging saliva with someone, even if it involved family or my best friend from school, Tonja.

Tonja was an Italian girl with black curls and the sweetest nature on earth, so pretty, and I loved her to bits. Her family was quite poor, and mine was quite alright with money. We knew that because of our clothes and our school equipment was quite different, so we swapped our coats and shoes sometimes.

Still, even if I loved my dearest friend Tonja to bits, I had the following problem: When I had one of these mini Tetra-packs with orange juice with me. Whenever she wanted a sip, I would always have to give the whole juice-box to her because the sheer thought of our spit mixing in my mouth made my stomach turn around. I didn't want her, or anyone else's saliva in my drink or my mouth. Sucking on the same straw was disgusting – Ewww, gross!

As if it happened yesterday, I can recall a situation where Tonja and I are standing in front of the gymnasium. She is eating an apple, I tell a joke. She has to laugh and spits a tiny bit of apple on my chest. I look at it and instantly have to throw up a little bit on the stairs. Tonja is in shock, so am I, and we quickly make our way back into the classroom, not losing a word over it. Later, the teacher complains about a "pig" that soiled the stairs, and while I am sweating blood, Tonja is giving me a wink, and we keep our little secret. "Thank God," I thought, "What would the others think of me? That would be so embarrassing…"

I would also throw up involuntarily for emotional reasons as a reaction to emotional stress. I, for example, got sick when I had to lie. I just couldn't do it. I got tummy cramps and went green and pale.

I remember that my brother once stole an extra toy attached to a kiddie magazine so that I could have one, too. I appreciated his sweet intention of wanting to share it with me, but I developed a fever and a stomach bug because I felt so bad about keeping this secret. All I could think of was my brother going off the right path and me supporting him. I spun it out to my brother ending up in prison one day. Leaning over a bucket, crying, I finally told my mum the truth, and my stomach bug was instantly cured. This particular low tolerance to certain stressors was not only related to worldly guilt, but also my firm belief in God and the divine laws – as in "thou shalt not lie!".

My faith was, by the way, another strangeness I was born with because God was not really a theme in our home. We did not pray together, and we didn't talk much about God or go to a lot to church as a family, but I LOVED church at school, and above all, I loved God, Jesus, and all the Saints and angels. I sang in the Dom (that's the name of our cathedral) in the choir, and the elementary school I went to was part of a Catholic abbey. My parents had picked these places based on convenience because everything was in walkable distance. The way my teachers and priests taught us about religion was very innocent and sweet, and I always had the feeling that God was my best friend and took care of me. There was never the "hell-fire-education-style" that so many other people in the world have to endure.

The dark side of dogma can make us sick for life when teachings of sin, hell, and damnation are part of the religious doctrine.

But thankfully, God was my friend and always with me. I prayed every night for my family and to say thank you for all the blessings in life. I do not know why. My brother went to the same schools but always remained, just like my parents, weirded out by my spiritual life.

Pieces of the puzzle are emerging again: the pattern of being the odd one out - the weirdo. But as you know, I see things very differently today. Instead of perceiving myself as weird, whiny, or bad because it made me throw up when people drank from my straw or when I had to lie, I now interpret my issues at the time like this: I was an extraordinarily sensitive and susceptible kid. I was gifted with a heightened sense of awareness, empathy, and justice.

Being a reactive receptacle to this world's impulses is the perfect gift if used right - it is the wood that art and new ways of thinking get carved out of. But back then, this sensitivity, which was untrained and misunderstood at the time, felt more like a hazard, than a gift. Nonetheless, as my confidence was still half-way intact, my perception of being different and not precisely fitting in was probably the first small gate that I subconsciously locked for myself, mainly because I didn't know better. I just wanted to fit the mold.

LOSING MY PERFECTION

~ The Machine Must be Broken ~

My heightened sensitivity had its benefits, too: I was a straight-A student and the teachers favorite, and despite my nervous and quirky tendencies, I was quite respected among peers.

Even though I was thin-skinned, I was courageous and had a strong sense of justice and a heart for outsiders. I also had the guts to defend myself, if necessary, sometimes even with fists. I knew I could count on myself, and when I got angry, there was a good reason for it. When the rare occasion arose that something truly unacceptable occurred, it would turn me into a warrior of what was right, like when I had my first experience with bullying.

Usually, I had no issues putting bullies in their place. My brother had been a bully victim, and I remember giving his torturers intense lectures. But, this one in our class was a different caliber: Her name was Tina.

Tina lived in the social council block across from the beautiful 300-year-old house where we lived. Unlike Tina's home, ours overlooked the beige and green building sins of the '70s like a princess castle, including the velvety roses in their red lush, slinging their thorny arms as high as the second floor, almost up to my window. Tina and I had first been friends. She was a good looking, tall, and strong girl with reddish hair and freckles, looking a bit like Pippi Longstocking and equipped with charm and a good sense of humor. But shortly after we started 3rd grade, she began to behave strangely. Something terrible must have happened during the six weeks summer holidays. Rumor had it that her daddy was now in prison - for murder.

At the start of the new school year, Tina had picked an unusual candidate to sit next to: Svetlana. Svetlana was even taller than Tina but twice as dense. Her hair was reddish, too, but her shade was more on the orange/albino spectrum and sheered short, which made her look like a boy. She was not the brightest crayon in the box, and quite crude. On top of her strange look and questionable intelligence, she also had this strong lisp.

So far, I had gotten on well with Svetlana, too. As mentioned, I used to make no difference between outsiders or the "cool kids," and that attitude had always served me well. Where Tina's and Svetlana's sudden friendship came from, since Tina had mocked Svetlana many times in the past, seemed strange to me.

Soon I would find out Tina's true motives: she seemed to groom Svetlana into something like an "Igor-character", the lab-assistant to many Gothic villains - a subservient, blindly executing troll-like persona under the spell of her master.

Within a few weeks, the two of them developed a new regime in class, where Tina gathered all the girls except Tonja and me around her during recess. Next, she would take a good look at their sandwiches. She would then pick the most delicious looking one and eat it. Who had anything against it would get a punch in the stomach from Svetlana, who would make her sandwich pick of the day right after Tina.

I found it bizarre that the girls went with it, but was more bemused than anything at the time. The next change that Tina and Svetlana implemented was that, as soon as the bell rang for recess, a selection of girls would pack up Tina's school bag and books and bring it to wherever the next class was. Six other girls would carry Tina. Yes. Tina herself was carried around like Cleopatra, the queen of Egypt. I remember wondering if I was the only one to think that this was hideous? Svetlana caught me while I stared at the spectacle in bewilderment and gave me a shove. "Got a problem?" I answered, "Yes, I do. I have never seen such a ridiculous scene in my life," and walked away.

When I came to school the next day, the seat next to me was empty. When I looked across the room, I saw Svetlana sitting to Tina's right, waving at me with a sarcastic smile and left to Tina was, yes, exactly: Tonja. They had gotten to her, too. I thought: "Enough is enough," but I acted as if it was the most ordinary day at school. Inside, however, I was incredibly disappointed in Tonja. What had they threatened her with? Whatever it was, it was time to come up with a plan.

For the next few days after school, I visited every girl that was in Tina's "army" at home. I brought candy and sat down with them, asking them how they felt about the new ways at school. Most of them cried and thanked me for taking the initiative to come over, trying to help. I proposed that we should all stick together and that that would make us untouchable. I explained that I wasn't interested in war with Tina or Svetlana. I just wanted my friend Tonja back sitting next to me and that this reign of fear and kicks in the stomach would end. The girls, one by one, were all thrilled and hopeful about my suggestion, and we planned to all meet 15 minutes before school to welcome Tina and Svetlana as a united front. I assured them that I was happy to be the one to talk to the two of them and that things would be alright.

The next day, I woke up excited and anxious, ready to bring all this behind all of us. When I was turning into the last alley that would lead straight to school, I suddenly sensed something strange. I looked around and saw the head of one of the girls I had talked to hide behind a wall quickly.

I knew right then that my plan had backfired. Sure enough, a minute later, I would turn my head again and saw all the girls walking behind me like an angry grey wall with feet – led by Svetlana and Tina in the front.

Something strange happened at that moment. Instead of being afraid, I became calm and ready for whatever was about to happen next, which was that the whole group behind me speeding up to attack me. Trying to not come across as being afraid, I continued at my original pace and maintained a steady, monotonous walking rhythm when I received Tina's first hard shove from behind. I stopped and took a deep breath through my nostrils.

Not even looking at her, I calmly whispered to Tina: "Keep your sticky fish-stick-fingers off of me." An even harder second shove from behind followed that miraculously didn't make me move an inch or lose my balance or calm.

She screamed: "I DON'T HAVE STICKY FISH-STICK-FINGERS, YOU STUPID COW!" Again, I took a deep breath and turned my head a little to take a look at her hand that had pushed me now twice. I repeated precisely the same line, but this time I was way more sincere: "Keep your sticky fish-stick-fingers off of me." Tina screamed even louder than she had before, also, precisely the same line: "I DO NOT HAVE STICKY FISH-STICK-FINGERS, YOU STUPID COW!"

Then the third push followed, but this time it was a full bodyweight effort on Tina's side.

I was able to catch it in a way that I only had to move one single gracious step forward without shaking, stumbling, or falling. This time, I turned around and looked her straight in the eye and said, centered, yet with force: "I say it one more time, keep your STICKY FISH-STICK-FINGERS OFF OF ME." This time she screamed: "I CAN PUT MY STICKY FISH-STICK-FINGERS WHEREVER I WAAAANT!" I gently smiled and returned to my calm self: "You see? You DO have sticky fish-stick-fingers - you just admitted it yourself."

A beat of utter silence among all of us, including Svetlana and the girls staring at us with their dropped jaws, followed. I turned around and walked off to school without further ado or looking around again.

Thank goodness the school was right there, so there was no time for anyone to lynch me after this. I felt as if God had protected me and blessed me with this almost comedic scene that I had experienced just now. I walked into the classroom and told the teacher that we had a big problem that we all needed to talk through.

Now, finally, my emotions streamed out of me as I took chair by chair to the middle of the room. Hot tears mixed with so much disappointment ran over my face as everyone silently entered the classroom.

As soon as we sat down in the circle, my teacher asked if there was something that we needed to talk through. Crickets. Unresponsiveness from everyone. Our teacher finally asked me if I wanted to start the conversation, and I got up and replied: "You know, Mrs. Fisher, I think I'm ready to go home now. I am sure that this bunch of cowards can explain to you very well what has just happened out there and what Tina and Svetlana have been doing to all of us during the last weeks. I leave you to it because I want nothing more to do with it anymore." Then I took my bag and walked home without waiting for an answer.

To my surprise, there was no consequence for me leaving like that, only a concerned teacher calling my mum after school to ensure that I was alright.

Mrs. Fisher, my teacher asked my mum to let me know that order was re-established and if anything like that should happen again, I should come and talk to her. Indeed, the next day, everything was back to the old ways. Tonja was sitting next to me, asking me with "googly eyes" for forgiveness, and no one ever talked about the incident again.

Hint: Skeleton-Key-piece in sight! This time, I want to draw your attention to a positive memory that is deeply ingrained in my mind. Being an expert of myself doesn't mean to focus just on all the negative, but rather to look at the complete package.

Focusing on our milestones and our success stories helps us to remember who we are when we get lost in moments of self-doubt and when unhelpful "shitsdoms" pop up in our minds. More about that in-depth at a later point. The message here: One can be sensitive, YET COURAGEOUS. One can be an outsider, BUT THAT CAN ALSO BE A LEADER QUALITY.

Most importantly, whatever we did in our past or whatever we overcame like a hero, we have to bring back up and remember when we feel down.

Hitting fourth grade would bring new challenges. School wise, everything was still going smoothly, and I would remain a straight A-student.

But suddenly, I noticed that something I had no control over was changing: my body. I did not like it at all. I already thought of myself as being a little bit on the chubby side as a child. Not much, but I was a girl with a tiny little potbelly. I didn't feel ugly (yet), though.

I had beautiful hair. I liked my face, particularly my eyes and lips, and I also had long, sporty legs to make up for my shortcomings around the waistline. Still, no matter how hard I tried to build myself up, the thing in the middle with the sunken hole in it would never become my friend. I considered it as wobbly.

At ten years old, however, when my breasts started growing, I suddenly felt like a ridiculous duck. My hair, lips, and legs weren't enough anymore to make up for THAT.

Because I got frightened by the changes in my body, I had to deliver in other areas.

My parents, the dear people, saw a lot of different talents in me, and they were very supportive. My schedule was tight: tennis, piano, choir, ballet, jazz dance, and later on solo singing tuition. Regarding my bulimia, I think ballet belongs undeniably on the trigger-lists, no doubt. I loved to dance, but unlike the other girls, I dreaded looking at myself in the mirror for too long. I felt that most of the girls were thinner than I was. If that was true, I do not even know.

My eyes would only focus on what I didn't want to see, squeezed in white lycra and sequins. All the girls had the nice waist that carved in, but mine seemed to carve a little out, and, at best, when I was a little thinner, it was just as straight as my bum and my chest. I thought I was a walking rectangular cardboard with a potbelly in tights and a white leotard.

Because I wanted to have a waist, I remember sewing a 3-inch rubber band into some sort of belt and put it under my leotard. This self-made waist cincher was supposed to keep in my swim-ring. Well, you can't say that I wasn't creative.

Today, I honestly have to laugh about it. I was just a sweet and crazy bum, who worried about what other people thought of me way too much. The urge to compare myself to skinnier girls was a toxic gift related to implemented worries of "what others might think." Yes, shitsdom-alert! Please erase and re-wire if you find this kind of second-hand negative thought pattern in your system.

Within our extended family, we were all highly competitive among ourselves. Everyone compared their kids, their husbands and wives, their jobs, their achievements, and their looks all the time.

There was an innate vibe of either jealously or superiority that I grew up with, and that added to my self-destructive urge to compare myself in ways that would just end up in me feeling bad about myself. Competitiveness like that only ever leads to unhappiness.

Thank goodness that I discovered a powerful mantra. This magic spell can dissolve this self-harming way of thinking: the wonderful shitsdom antidote, the brilliant so-called "SO WHAT"-attitude. This two-word sentence should go into the mold of your key, btw. It's a great one. The very same line became a big friend of mine, and we experienced many time-travels to the past to gently laugh at the tiny muffin top of a 10-year old that was so utterly heartbroken because of it. SO WHAT. Humor paired with the "So-What-attitude" is, as far as I found out, a perfect combination of key-elements (literally). Remember, not dark humor, but a kind of shoulder-shrugging, head shaking, smirking, and forgiving humor.

Sometimes people can't help themselves in a better way, and they develop the most peculiar tools to cope with their lives during this strange sickness, like me and my teenage waste-band. Well, all I can say is thank God that time passes, and sooner or later, it is over, and we can say good-bye and forget about it.

Not everyone in my family was willing or able to overcome all personal pain and transform it into a brightly shining torch of love, though. Meet one very bitter example and also one of my more destructive influencers: meet my grandmother Kari. From early on, I had the impression that Oma Kari was a thoroughly unhappy woman.

Today I feel sorry for her. I have nothing but love for her. (Mind you, I doubt that she cares anyway because she passed away a long time ago.)

Oma Kari was part of the lost generation that was a young teenager when Adolph Hitler came into power. If you want to find out more about this madness and my grandmother's generation, go online and watch Adolf Hitler speaking to the Hitler Youth, the Hitlerjugend, in the Olympia stadium: pure horror.

All these naïve and brainwashed kids, who took this insane man and his lies as serious as bread to eat, and air to breathe. What would I do with my life if I had been a pubescent leader of the Hitler girls "BDM" (Bund Deutscher Maedchen / Union of German Girls) at the age of thirteen, thinking I was part of something fantastic? Only to realize a few years later, that I actively participated in a system that committed the crimes of the holocaust, the mass killing that Hitler called ethnic cleansing. I can't imagine how that must have been - carrying this kind of guilt and to be silent about it... a scary and dreadful thought.

People of Grandma Kari's generation had no real identities anymore. That part of history was silenced. We all know why. There is simply nothing that can be said in defense. So, there she was, a bitter, disenchanted and unhappy woman, a strict mom to her son and a strict grandmother too, but I loved her nevertheless.

Grandma Kari had a vast collection of shitsdoms and blew my mind when it came to be harsh and not exactly kiddie-friendly. Like that one time that I came to visit for a few weeks in the summer holidays between 3rd and 4th grade. My parents dropped me off with a suitcase and left.

I looked forward to staying with my grandparents because grandma Kari wasn't the only one waiting there for me: My Granddad, Opa Wolli, who had taken on the role of the "good cop" in their partnership, was there, too! Opa Wolli was, in many ways, the counter opposite to Oma Kari. He was the "good cop," the fun guy, and took my brother and me out on endless walks "into the wide world." He could cook like a king and be full of jokes, music, and games, but he also had a temper and quite a foul mouth. I loved him so much.

Opa Wolli would make the days so fun-filled with bike rides in the park and other outings that the time away from home would fly by in a flash, and grandma Kari's grumpy nature was a minor issue.

Entering their apartment, I shook hands with my granny to say hi, as one does if one wants to be polite. Instead of following up with a hug and a "welcome, sweet-heart", she took my little paw, stared at it for a second, frowned, and said: "You have fat hands." I said: "What? That's not true - hands cannot be fat, granny. And also, I am only ten years old, and you shouldn't say that to me," She said: "Oh yes. You have fat hands. We are going to put you on a diet. I don't want your parents to think that I'm stuffing you here."

And then she put me on a diet. And I had to weigh myself in front of her every evening. It was grandma's mission. I was not too fond of her stupid weight loss program and all her comments about me, insinuating that I lacked disciple or wasn't looking right. I remember feeling ashamed of myself and my body.

The first worries about my body image that I had experienced in ballet class had now been made official by my grandmother: NOW I DID NOT IMAGINE IT, I WAS TOLD THAT I NEEDED TO LOSE WEIGHT.

Grandma Kari surely didn't have a clue what sorrow her diet would bring onto me, but these sentences would fester and stay a long time in my sub-conscience. I would mistake them soon as my own voices in the head.

CLUE! Remembering this particular holiday at grandma Kari's was like a light bulb of great consequence going off in my head during my recovery process. It was undeniably significant on my way back to health. Because once I dug it out of my foggy memory, I realized a whole collection of other people's shitsdoms in my head!

Note to self: most of the voices in our heads, especially the horrible ones, are not our even our own voice. If we do not consciously look inward and listen to them with non-judgmental and non-reactive peace and patience, we cannot detect and dissect them because they are deeply buried and ancient.

"You have fat hands" had remained in my sub-consciousness for a long time, before I became an accomplished, scientific yet self-loving reader of my mind and life.

Back home again, right after I experienced my first diet, my 4th grader school-life took on a strange shape, as well. Because I was so ahead of everyone else, I became a bit annoying with my permanently raised hand, and the teachers would now send me outside to look after the tomatoes in the abbey garden until the end of the year - they didn't know what to do with me anymore. I seemed to know everything and probably made the rest of the class feel as if they were behind.

We all survived it, and I got to do a lot of gardening and left primary school on an absolute high, believing I was unstoppable and ready to change the world with my brains. The switch to middle school followed a year later. After I was identified as highly gifted via an IQ test, my parents were called in for a meeting. With a thin-lipped, annoyed undertone, the lady who my parents had that meeting with, a teacher whose own daughter was also in my class but had not been identified as profoundly gifted, put my parents straight back in their place: "Well, well. Please do not make a big thing of it. A lot of children are special here."

Lines, coming from a jealous teacher who couldn't get over the fact that her daughter did not score in the profoundly gifted realms at that same test.

Because my parents are both teachers, they didn't question another snippy teacher's opinion but were somewhat intimidated. They also found the idea of enrolling me in a gifted school 30 minutes away from home overwhelming.

Only much later, I would find out about what ever happened to that test and my actual score. I was furious when I heard that there would have been the option to go to a specialized school that would have nurtured my talents better. You will find out in a bit, why.

CLUE! Knowing your outliers, strengths, or weaknesses alike is a fabulous analytics tool. If you were not supported when you needed it, If you didn't receive the recognition, when you deserved it, please go back in time and give your mini-me the hugs and praise he/she earned but never got.

Supporting your inner child is a brilliant way to release old feelings of inadequacy or injustice. I cried when I tried this out for the first time after I read about it in a self-help book and have stepped back in time on numerous occasions. It works.

By the way, I think this is an excellent point to stop pointing out hints and clues. I think you got the hang of it by now.

The pace of the new school was intimidating. I was used to the easy life from elementary school, where teachers would leave me alone if I had advanced knowledge. Not so there.

In addition to needing to study a lot more, I also had to do so much homework! In elementary school, doing homework had been a 5 minutes job.

Now all of this took a few hours. My artistic hobbies came out of a balance almost in an instant. Not only was there no time for practicing the piano, but also no time to play the flute, or paint either. Instead, continually nagging guilt about my homework juxtaposed to me not wanting to do it took up a lot of my headspace. It felt stuck in my head.

While I experienced severe trouble in transitioning to this prestigious middle school, I found it impossible to communicate this block in my head, especially to my parents, the teachers. I began to wonder if all of my new negative emotions revolving around the school were the result of being spoiled?

Had I received too many toys, too much good food and intellectual stimulation, jazz, theatre, classical music, and beautiful clothes? Had I turned out to be a lazy brat, full of myself, yet incapable of keeping up with doing all this homework? Or was I, contrary to what I believed in before, stupid after all?

The feeling of being perfect broke away on multiple ends, not only intellectually.

A doctor came to school to check our health and examined our bodies, checked our eyes, ears, weight, and teeth. I was so proud of my pearly-whites and cleaned them three times a day. After I just had received lovely compliments for my teeth, I remember having to sit down and look into one of these machines for checking my eyesight. I did my best and expected the same reaction I just had encountered regarding my teeth. With a confident smile, I asked the doctor: "And? All good? Can I go now?" The doctor responded: "Yes, and you need glasses."

Blood was rushing through my cheeks, and I swallowed hard: "What? Excuse me, Mr., but I can see perfectly well! There must be something wrong with the machine. Could we please repeat the test?" We repeated the vision exam, and I tried harder to see these little circles that had a piece missing, one time on the top, on the left, on the bottom (…or maybe not?), whatever. And then I was sent home with a prescription for a pair of glasses, crying.

My parents, both proud owners of frameless specs, took me to an optician and ordered the frameless version they had for little ones. Ugh. I was miserable and instead of feeling like an ugly duck, I felt like an ugly old owl from now on. I didn't tell my parents how much I hated my new glasses because they meant it so well and spent so much money on them. Frameless models are costly.

My particular model was custom created for my face to supposedly make me look beautiful, which I did not notice. But they were so fragile and would break so damn often, too. Time after time, I would accidentally sit, sleep, or step on them, and when that happened, I would get into significant trouble.

Sometimes I even stuck the glass together with a piece of sticky tape and got away with hiding them for a week or so, but sooner or later, I got caught. My new friend from school, Cindy, had a pink frame with little red dots. I was jealous and wanted to look cute, and trendy like her. I subtly indicated that I would prefer Cindy's glasses to mine, but my parents reacted quite hurt, as expected. They explained their good intentions to me as if I didn't know them already.

Today I know that the way to hell is paved with good intentions. A year after having broken or lost my glasses once again, I switched seats to the front row of my class and stopped wearing them for good after that. Squinting my eyes seemed a much better option in my (short-sighted) eyes than the unsexy nonsense with my disaster glasses.

Since that time, I have observed a lot of children, including my own: They are clear in what they want or what they don't want and don't doubt their wholeness too much.

As we grow older, we lose chunks of this confidence step by step and all the time, mainly when we haven't found our tribe yet. It is an important observation to make for human beings to doubt and question themselves and to realize that they are not the center of the universe.

But why do some of us never stop to allow the negative observations to be so intense and out of balance that they make us forget the good? One under-lying character trait of people prone to self-destructive behaviors such as addictions and EDs is having a highly sensitive and critical mind, which is a sign of high intelligence.

The question is: are the desires to achieve and succeed bad? There is nothing wrong with those wants. But the disruption of these perfect ideas is always around the corner, ready to test our innate idealism.

The world is, in many ways, a dense and rough place. Obstacles to overcome are all around. Feeling overwhelmed, not being able to change, not being able to speak our truth to the ones we love, being put on a diet, feeling fat, or believing that we look like an old, ugly owl, are included on that list of hurdles. Even if we were perfect at all times, we would still have to cope with all the mess happening on a global level, like natural catastrophes, accidents, global warming, wars, starving children, cancer, theft, and corrupt politicians. It is some tough work here on planet earth, especially for our heads.

One thing is for sure: THIS CHAOTIC WORLD IS MOST CERTAINLY NOT MEANT TO BE PERFECT.

56

At the same time, we live in a universe of balance and harmony. This world is cause and effect based. Without the problems, there would be no evolution, no development, no growth, and no expansion. Everything is in constant flow and develops, develops, develops, and that is the most beautiful, logical response to human struggle of never being perfect enough: Nothing is naturally perfect, because otherwise, we would face a dull, sleepy, stagnant place. Growth, change, i.e., life, would be impossible.

A HARSH AWAKENING

~ Bushmen, Lightning, and Spit in my Face ~

Taking your first flights out of the nest to find out who you are as an individual can be rough. You can fall without anything to cling to if no one is there who understands what you are going through. Oh boy!

Let's mark it right here, that significant, anarchic, and pimply milestone: HELLO, PUBERTY. Everything turned around, upside down.

Being difficult and different suddenly became my second skin, instead of embarrassing!

On top of bad skin, growing breasts, and the first period, it sank in that life would never be as chilled out as it had been before in elementary school. After all the excitement of being in a new school and meeting all these new kids, I began to miss my old friends and felt lonely and disconnected. Tonja went to a different school now.

I wouldn't have a close female friend for many years to come. I mean a BFF that would love me and that I could trust. For a girl, it is crucial to have an awesome FEMALE friend to be happy and to feel understood. I was on the lookout, but people seemed different at this school, more reserved and competitive.

The one that would come closest to being my new BFF was the girl with the cute glasses that I so desperately wanted to have myself: Cindy. We sat next to each other. Cindy was like a ray of light. She was all cheekiness and a pinch of sweet naivety. She had the blonde hair of a sun-kissed field in late summer, a perfectly tiny nose, turquoise-colored eyes with a copper dash in the middle, the loveliest figure with that perfect waist, a cute apple bottom and the skin of a peach. It was fun to be with Cindy. At the same time, I never knew what she thought about anything or anyone, including me. Her own opinion hid under that Cindy-typical, everlasting smile and her perpetual politeness.

Cindy was the first person at whose house I was allowed to stay over for a sleepover. At her place, we would share our latest discoveries in music and make-up or exchange fashion tips that we found in teenager-magazines. We were heavily into those. Stories of first physical experiences with boys like kissing or handholding would soon follow. Our confessions were, of course, accompanied by lots of giggling and whispering. But for some reason, it stayed on the surface.

The fondness I felt for spending time at Cindy's place was not only because of her. I thought that her mother was the nicest and coolest mom ever, too. In comparison to my mum, Cindy's mum seemed to be so much more relaxed, more like a friend than an authority.

The emphasis here is on SEEMED. I was admittedly very impressionable back then and bought into the happiness. The reality behind her mask of awesomeness was, however, bleak and tragic: Cindy's mother had just gotten through a divorce, and Werner, Cindy's mother's new husband, had just moved in. What nobody knew and what I would only find out much later as an adult, was that Cindy's mum had her own battles with addiction. That would lead to several nervous breakdowns, and as far as I know, suicide attempts, but back then, the illusion was immaculate. I didn't have a clue that there might be something wrong.

The first semester was almost over when Cindy and I decided to join our school's rowing team. We ended up rowing together in a double.

Our dedication and team spirit would be rewarded soon, and we won a few regional competitions. I remember our first race and us rowing as if we were chased by the great white shark. We won by 20 lengths, oh my!

Cindy and I seemed to be a real dream team, unfortunately only when it came to sports and teenage magazines. Something that started to bug me was that she never seemed to stand up for me, which would soon play an important role.

Recognition and re-assurance by others are invaluable, especially for young folks, no matter how strong one comes across. Everyone needs and deserves it. As an adult, I made it part of my "true friendship checklist" that my friends need to be inspirational to me and nurture my well-being as much as I nurture theirs. I do not want to blame Cindy for the lack of empathy when it came to my needs.

Poor Cindy. She was just putting up a brave face while she was dealing with her family problems hailing down on her, unnoticed by anyone. I have compassion for her today and have held on to this old friendship fondly in my heart - even if we haven't seen each other for over 25 years. Aren't we all in the same boat, just trying to fit in and to be loved?

Much worse than not being able to bond in a carefree way with your best friend was what happened next: I became an atheist.

It is quite mind-boggling to me that I can pinpoint the actual start of a meltdown that would eventually make me stick my finger down the throat. My whole outlook on life and my every thought would soon turn around when I was losing my faith in God.

I had just turned thirteen, when a book-smart boy in my class who I respected, would make the following statement in physics class: "Religion is for primitives. It is a naive delusion, and an uneducated try to give the un-explicable a reason. When thunder burned a tree, the ancient bush-people said: "OUHHH! That was God," because they didn't know anything about physics and electric fields in the clouds that cause thunder. Religion is for stupid and superstitious people who can neither reason scientifically, nor think sophisticated thoughts."

This "thesis" (i.e., shitsdom) stuck with me for some reason. Having experienced a few bubbles burst in front of my eyes regarding my self-image and perfection, it kind of slipped through those cracks and festered.

It also fitted to the feelings of loneliness that I harbored in my heart. Soon after my first doubts, I began to wonder if I was only praying to myself at night. Did those prayers only feel so soothing because I reflected on positive things? Had I brainwashed myself? All worldly evil came to my mind, and all the imperfections and the unfairness, the tragedies and pains around us, and I tried desperately to make sense. But no matter how I tossed and turned, I couldn't find a solid answer to why there were dying children and so much injustice in the world. And why on earth did we have to die anyway? And lose everything sooner or later?

After a few weeks of heavy pondering upon the existence of God, I concluded that I should give up my old beliefs until I would find an answer to the senseless problems in the world. Comparing it to the experience of a sad wake-up, I concluded that death was the chemical end of the body and bodily functions. From now on, death was black - nothingness.

I now believed that heaven was an invention by the people who believed in Santa: idiots. Now that there was no heaven anymore, nothing made sense. I asked myself why we were here and why we were supposed to do good and show the other cheek. I couldn't find a plausible answer. God's mysterious plan suddenly seemed like a random play of nature, and whatever we did with our time was pointless anyway. If our existence was futile, the responsibilities are meaningless, too.

I further concluded that I might as well just make up my own rules if life was a random bubble floating between nothingness and oblivion. From now on, I was the sad and lonely center of my universe. No God to look up to for guidance anymore. I didn't know any better, and any other proper guidance was sparse and hard to come by, especially at school.

My religion teacher was a bland, elderly lady with a horn on her head, which she tried to cover with a strand of hair. Sometimes, when the windows were open in class, the wind would blow her hair to the other side and expose the horn. We would all look at each other and smirk. This was definitely not a go-to person for me.

Instead of confiding my doubts, I decided to make a game out of questioning her in class to the point where she blamed whatever she wasn't able to answer to the inexplicability of God. In my eyes and the eyes of my classmates, it was such a blatant cop-out. I was clearly winning every word match. Because of that, I suddenly felt for the first time some kind of weird satisfaction when I ridiculed my teacher to her face or behind her back.

My teacher would serve as the door opener for starting to clown around, using others as a target, something I had never done before. I realized that especially the condescending bully remarks, and the dirty jokes worked well with my classmates. Declaring war to any existing system, was fun!

Soon, I began to challenge everyone, involving these poor people in endless debates about nothing. I was just not in the right place. Deep down, I felt unhappy, and I desperately tried to feel empowered and to make friends.

My parents, as you can imagine, had the shock of their lives when I turned around 180 degrees like that. Gone was the little angel with braided hair, the straight A's, the sweet, caring girl that couldn't lie and was always friendly and polite.

The dawn of an absolute free fall at school was initiated as well. What I was about to experience right after the summer holidays would turn into the ideal breeding-condition for my ED.

To my own surprise, I had been looking forward to seeing a few people after the six-week summer break, and I caught myself awaiting the first day of school with eager anticipation. There was Ben, who I had an on-going fun flirt with (you will hear more about him later), and there was Matthew, another boy in my class who I felt more of some sort of platonic affection for. And there was, of course, Cindy, my friend that was so very different to me in many regards, not just because of the glasses our mums allowed us to wear (or not to wear).

At the beginning of that new school year and grade, we were expecting our new class teacher. In the past, we had been lucky with Mr. Fuller, a married, middle-aged, lovely man with two kids, who taught Latin and Sports and who was also our rowing coach. He was a great man with a mature, intelligent attitude who had guided us through the first year of middle school with a loving hand. We were sad about having to let him go, but the rules were the rules.

On this very first day, in this very first hour of school, there was this significant change about to happen, and we were utterly curious, who our new teacher would be. It was a big deal, and I recall looking forward to it. I was one of the first students in the class.

I picked out a good seat and put my scarf on the chair next to me to reserve it for Cindy, who wasn't there yet. The room slowly filled up, and the minute arm of the clock on the wall moved closer and closer to the full hour. I started to get a little anxious because Cindy wasn't there yet. Would Cindy make it on time to get the seat next to me that I tried to keep free for her?

CLUE: Smells like there is a little EMPATH at work, who is getting anxious about her best buddy not getting into trouble! There is an undeniable connection between being an empath, who takes on the stress, and pain of others, and addiction. Are you an empath? Keep on asking that question. It is the greatest gift, but if you don't know about it, it will become your downfall, and you end up living the fear of others.

Back to that first class of the year that would turn my life topsy-turvy: In our school, it was considered a miserable tone to come late to class, especially to the first one after the holidays, and I didn't want Cindy to start like that.

More and more people asked me if they could sit next to me. I got up and anxiously waited at the door, trying to spot her in the hallway.

Exactly one minute before the bell would ring, at 7:59 am, an older, skinny man with huge glasses, dressed as if he had just had run away from a 50's movie set, entered the room. I held the door for him. He didn't look at me and behaved rather anxious and unfriendly.

There – finally! I spotted Cindy at the end of the hallway and waved at her. She ran towards me as the bell rang, and I waited until she slipped in so I could show her where I had reserved our seats.

I quietly closed the door and watched as Cindy, heavily panting, sat down. I winked at her, and she threw me a grateful smile when all of a sudden hell broke loose.

All I remember is hearing this new teacher SCREAM at me so that the whole room shook: "AND YOUUUU! WHO DO YOU THINK YOU ARE THAT YOU DARE TO COME EVEN A SECOND LATE?!"

He grabbed my arm and pulled me towards his front desk. You could hear a pin drop. Everyone stared at me in shock. Literally, all jaws had dropped.

While he went on with his rant, he furiously wrote his name, Dr. Oxblood, on the blackboard with a squeaking noise. He aggressively underlined it twice. Once he was finished, he looked at me as if I had just signed my own death warrant, and threw the piece of chalk in my face.

I wanted to explain that I had been there the whole time and that I had held the door open for him, couldn't he remember? But I was unable to get a single word out because he interrupted me furiously after the first peep. Now, he addressed the whole class, still screaming like a mad man, showering me with his saliva (as you know, I had this particular thing about saliva - ahh!). He explained that from now on, he would use me as an example to show the whole class what would happen if they dared not to behave. Then he wrote my name on the blackboard, again with that dreadful noise, and said that I was a stupid person for trying to provoke him and I shouldn't believe that I was smart. He would prove that people like me who dared to come late or backchat in his class were even too stupid to count to three. He continued that he "knew" students like me and promised that he would prove that I had fooled other teachers and that I would fail in his class. Holy cow! What just happened to me?

Mr. Oxblood went on for about fifteen minutes about how he was going to make sure that people listen and respect him, and repeated over and over how he was going to show them that it was better not to be like me. This guy was nuts.

Just a few months before that, this incident would have made me break down in tears because it was so rude and unjust. But I just sat there. I was frozen. I swore to myself not to show any weakness at all, the only handle on the situation I had at that moment.

It was such a bizarre scenario that I almost had to laugh out loud myself. I couldn't believe that this man was serious and that he just wouldn't stop. This was a proper adult tantrum! Some of his remarks even reminded me of my own sarcastic sense of humor at the time.

Looking back, I don't know how someone like Mr. Oxblood could have possibly become a teacher. It would soon become evident that he was excellent at math, but his teaching skills were borderline psycho. I thought this could just not be happening for real. Still under shock, I came home that first day of school, and I naturally told my parents about this experience, but they didn't grasp the extent of the absurdity I had just experienced. They must have thought that I dramatized the whole situation in a way that only teenager angst could exaggerate.

A few weeks of hell went by. Nothing blew over. Mr. Oxblood was proving his point and would ridicule or shame and verbally abuse me in the disguise of sarcastic jokes every single time we had math. And for the very first math test, he gave me the very first F in my life after I had been a top student all my life - just like he promised. He claimed that I had used the wrong method. When I asked my fellow students to help me, they, including Cindy, explained that they were scared to be next, but if matters should "get rough," "of course" they would help me.

I reached out to my old class teacher Mr. Fuller, and he agreed that Mr. Oxblood was a problematic character, but advised that it was best to keep quiet and to remain non-reactive. Nobody seemed to understand the severity of my dilemma. No matter how I worded it, I came across like a whining teenager that was just trying to blame the "bad teacher" for her shortcomings, as so many people do when they get bad grades. It is incomprehensible that this kind of abuse could happen in a school with such an excellent reputation, but it did. And I was right in the eye of the tornado.

Within the following months, I began to dislike my classmates for not backing me up. I despised them for laughing together with him out of fear, Schadenfreude, or relief that it wasn't them who were getting slaughtered five times a week. I lost respect for all of them, even my closest peers at the time, including Cindy.

They didn't seem to care less about my problems. Instead, they just continued to openly admit that they didn't want to mess with Mr. Oxblood and risk bad grades, while I got one after the next. What happened to their promise of stepping in when things would get rough? Could it get any worse? Everyone kept on saying, "keep your chin up." Thanks. That was all I was doing. It didn't help at all. Especially not when Cindy hid behind her book and giggled as another piece of chalk would land on my head. Ironically, I had always been the one to stand up for others. I couldn't understand how others were able to tolerate this abuse. I would have never allowed this to happen to someone else.

Maybe Mr. Oxblood could "smell" that about me. He was quite high up on the school's political ladder, probably because of his doctor title. After all, he was a respected mathematician, and he previously had taught at the university in Cologne. The other teachers at our school were immensely impressed with his credentials, but I, being the person who I am now, wonder WHY HE CHANGED SCHOOLS FROM UNIVERSITY TO MIDDLE SCHOOL IN A DIFFERENT TOWN?!

Being a teacher's daughter, I must admit that this looks fishy through my adult eyes. I am sure that I wasn't the first person to encounter abuse from this man. How sad that is.

His disturbed, sadistic behavior must have been something he must have experienced himself in his past. Otherwise, people don't turn out to be abusers. It's not entirely his fault, I reckon.

We are all victims of our surroundings and of how we were conditioned. If we don't break free, we stay enslaved to these conditions and become mentally ill like him. And me. I forgive him. There is no other choice for me. He is part of the human family just as much as I am. An ingenious idiot-savant character, excellent in one particular field, but otherwise pretty lost.

If you want to add a label, he surely had some sort of mental illness. Whatever it was, it was something not entirely healthy in the head, and the change to our school and my class must have frustrated him very much. And then there was me, a spoiled looking girl in flashy sneakers that she had doodled smiley faces on, trying to make sense of this world with a big invisible question mark on her forehead. I guess I was just merely a trigger for him like the combination of stress and hazelnut spread would become a trigger for me.

You might wonder where my parents were amidst all this? It's quite simple. After initially reaching out to them, I couldn't fathom to bother them again with this. Instead, I wanted to keep everything away from them. I avoided the topic because I couldn't bear to show them that I had received my first F. I didn't want to give this win to that crazy teacher to make my parents believe that I was stupid or lazy. My plan remained to sail through all this without causing my parents any stress. I was sure I could fix this sick joke along the way by writing satisfactory exams.

But the pressure, loneliness, and suppressed anger wore me down rapidly. Worst of all was that I felt that my dignity as a human being was under attack.

Because not one person recognized the trouble I was experiencing on a day to day basis, I decided to take matters in my own hands. I was sitting in my darkened room, sad to the core, dreading the thought of tomorrow's math class and the humiliation.

After a long pensive while, I took a piece of paper and began with a dry, fact-based calculation of my situation. I asked myself what would happen if I just wouldn't go to his classes. Could I go to only the minimum of lessons as necessary? He would surely give me that "F", that he had promised to me on day one, although I had been a good math student until that point.

I continued my chain of thoughts. So, given that I would have to handle that worst-case scenario, meaning getting an "F" indeed, I could simply level it out with an "A" in the other classes. That would severely drop my overall grade ratio, but I could make the year, and that was all I needed. All I had to do was to hold out for two years. Then we would get a new teacher, and I could make up for the bad overall ratio and go back to math classes. But how could I stay away without getting in trouble with school or my parents? A girl popped in my mind that was a few years higher up. She had a chronic illness and was partially home-schooled. It dawned on me: all I had to do was to invent a disease that could keep me from school at certain times. Especially those two-hour math-classes. The single hour classes were already bad enough, but during the double pack, there was too much time, and it was impossible to escape the man's offensive attacks.

He would always ask me to the blackboard when there was a new phenomenon or formula. Then, to his and the class' utter amusement, he would lead me in all possible pitfalls, he would ask me the most confusing and misleading questions and so on. It was some sort of sadistic, public torture. I had become the laughing stock of my math class. All I could do was to shut up, smile, and try to joke back; since I felt I had lost my dignity, my self-respect went away as well, thanks to being this man's favorite bully-victim.

I put my escape plan into action and invented chronic illnesses where I claimed to have infections or sudden seizures, all combined with a high risk of fainting. That enabled me to avoid Mr. Oxblood's classes while I could attend the other courses on that day. I needed to bring my A-game to German, French, Art, Biology, and Sports to level out my projected bad grades in math that I was about to earn without a doubt. I also needed to make sure that I wouldn't skip too many in a row. It needed to come across as natural and believable.

In record time, I became an expert in faking, forging, and fable-telling. As part of my dirty action plan, I stole a signed check from my mother and practiced her signature. After a few trials, I got the hang of it and "Bam," there it was, looking smooth and real as it rolled out of my wrist. That was easy.

After mastering my mother's signature, step two followed: her entire handwriting. Bingo! I got that down within 30 minutes of practice, too. More illegal actions like these followed. Inspired by stealing the check, I realized how easy it was to take money from my mom as well, and I happily helped myself to 5 Deutsche Mark (the old German currency). Wow, that was effortless, too. And so, I kept on taking 2 Marks here and 10 Mark there.

I would tell myself that I deserved it because a: my parents had not checked if there was truth to my complaints about that math teacher when all of this mess was in the beginning stages and b: they gave me the lousiest pocket money. Now I could at least afford a coke when I was hiding away in the café around the corner of my home. Because sometimes, I needed to bridge the time before coming home at one o'clock, pretending that I just came from school. My whole charade was a question of timing and acting.

I would start my skip-math-classes-day in the cathedral garden. I always took some books and homework with me to write poems and essays during these mornings, sitting in the grass that was still wet from the dew, feeling a little more self-worthy again. After all, I was doing actual school work during that time. And I had outsmarted everyone. I thought.

When parent-teacher conferences came up, I told my parents that the gatherings were either postponed or canceled. I couldn't believe how lucky I was to get away with it every time. Every crime that I successfully executed gave me new confidence. It felt good to become a master in manipulating my whole environment. Being back in charge was an incredible relief.

That period of my life was full of extreme developments. There was as much pain as there would be excitement: I got my first part in a play. Joining an acting ensemble probably saved me from falling deeper into my depression because it enriched my life with something extraordinary and fun. I finally had something tangible that I could hold on to, something that kept me sane. And the new crowd I found myself in was simply superb. The theatre group consisted of mainly older students. Only my pal Ben and I were younger, so nobody knew anything about my situation in class.

Everyone here respected me and valued what I had to say. For me, acting was, simply put, the best of all worlds. I remember the first time I ever acted. It felt as if a hammer had just hit me on the head. I instantly realized that this was exactly it – I was at home here, this is what I wanted, and it combined everything I loved! I probably had found my profession. One thing that sealed the deal for my love of acting was the deep and profound meaning of being an actor. Acting in plays was like being in philosophy heaven. I already had a collection of Immanuel Kant, David Hume, Socrates, Plato, Aldous Huxley, and many more were soon to follow.

Organizing an acting ensemble at our school, on the other hand, turned out to be hard labor - a labor of passion and love that none of our teachers had expressed for many previous years, until Mr. Davis, the philosophy teacher, had a heart. We were producing one of Jean-Paul Sartre's plays about the French resistance and the Vichy regime - some heavy material. My role was meaty, and I felt such liberation, expressing myself this way. I enjoyed the process of putting a play together. The political power in it. The music. The literature. Having a space to speak freely. The intense body-work like dancing, and the expression of extreme and subtle feelings, but especially the chance to allow my anger to come out in a channeled way, i.e., in a role was amazing.

New, happy, creative, and powerful feelings reemerged. From then on, at least from an artistic standpoint, I was on a high and got involved with as many theatre projects I could land. Simultaneously I also began to sing in a few bands. Suddenly, I wasn't the weirdo and laughing-stock anymore, I'd hang out with a popular and older crowd, and do cool, artsy stuff. To my parent's horror, that unfortunately also meant that I discovered the nightlife in our town with all its bars and dance clubs.

Within the next semester, the school had become that dreaded "other thing." The complexity of the confusing net of lies I had built, forced me to dismiss more classes than just math, to keep it all looking realistic. But I was busy now outside of school, and therefore I got sloppier, too. When it rained or when it was cold, and I couldn't face spending a whole day outside or in a café, I simply hopped back into bed as soon as my parents went out of the house. There was only one issue: my other grandmother, Oma Mimi, who lived in the apartment upstairs with my aunt. Every day, she would come down to make the beds and cook.

Needless to say, that now and then, she got me busted. Only one wrong word needed to slip out of her mouth when we were sitting together with my mum at the lunch table, and my mum knew what was up. When that happened, I was FURIOUS with poor old granny Mimi…

So sorry, my dearest dear-heart, you did not deserve how I treated you. One always offloads emotional rubbish at the closest and kindest folks. Oma Mimi was indeed my closest ally and the most loving person one can imagine. I was tired and worn out from my nightly activities with the more mature crowd. I ignored her sad eyes as my own would soon be disappearing behind a smoky (yes, I started smoking), and alcohol-drenched (yes, I started drinking), curtain before my eyes.

Crossing these kinds of boundaries was only the beginning, the tip of the iceberg that would freeze up underneath my feet, unseen by everyone, including myself.

LOVE IS A STRANGE THING

~ The Fata Morgana ~

Something unexpected and depressing had happened in my family while I was battling the Ox-blood-shed: we suddenly lost a big deal of money. Out of the blue, a very extensive tax audit took my father by surprise. It cost him 100,000 bucks.

Financially and emotionally, the four of us felt the difference immensely. I wasn't really allowed to talk about this issue, so I isolated myself even more than I already did. I knew by now how to withhold and store up my issues. School included. Instead, I focused even more on my other endeavors.

On stage and also on the water at the rowing club, I could shine as an artist or athlete. That made more sense than trying to hold on to my A-student past. At the same time, I could transform my anger and sadness into powerful monologues or rowing strokes.

On the rowing team, Cindy and I were about to start our training for the Youth Olympics.

Besides this excellent sportive opportunity and honor to participate, other exciting things were happening, down at the clubhouse at the river: One day, five boys from our school stepped out of the dressing rooms for males. What a very confusing and weirdly exciting surprise this was.

Suddenly, our training became even more appealing than it already was, and the rowing club turned into a sizzling hot-spot for flirtations and laughter. My hormones were cooking over. Eager to make more time for the club and these boys, I canceled my "stupid" ballet classes.

With my growing, muscular rowing physique, I now felt more like a buffalo among gazelles thanks to the absence of my waist paired with my freshly packed on back, neck, and calf muscles. (Side note: When I look back at old photos, I am shocked about how very much I did look like a gazelle myself. How warped my perception was thanks to being stuck in my head.)

At the club-house, the dirty jokes that I prided myself with came of good use, and my repertoire would expand quickly. There was so much new input from the boys. Especially one guy, David, who was a little short, but otherwise an incredibly likable, exciting, and funny person, left a lasting impression. It felt as if something had instantly "clicked" between us, and we became friends and began to spend time together beyond those short meetings at the club.

I remember David making me laugh so hard. He simply cracked me up whenever he opened his mouth. Life, all of a sudden, felt a lot more livable again.

Since David and I both lived in the same neighborhood, we had the same way home after the rowing afternoons. Ecstatically, I would push my green Holland bike next to him so that we could spend more time together. Oh, how I enjoyed those walks home.

Soon, we wouldn't want to stop the conversations that left us in stitches from all the giggling at his doorstep, and he invited me to come inside for a glass of juice. Once I had set foot in his house and met his lovely mum, sister, cat, and his blue budgie Herman, we made that juice quick-stop part of our rowing-club after hour ritual as well.

Time flew by, and I got to know my new friend better and better. I found out that David was a big prankster at school. He would always tell me his latest antics that he pulled with the teachers.

There was, for example, Mr. Walker, the strange and nerdy man who tried to explain the world of Physics to us at school, who happened to be one of David's favorite targets. David told me that Mr. Walker had a hearing aid, and as soon as Mr. Walker would enter the classroom, David would start to hum a high-pitched tune. This annoying, almost inaudible sound was just so perfectly subtle and irritating that Mr. Walker would always mistake it as a problem with his hearing aid. When the poor teacher would take it out his ear, shake and bang it against his wrist, the whole class would smirk and chuckle while David would continue his game.

Another favorite prank of his was to bring a universal remote control to school. David would get it out and rewind, stop and forward as he pleased, leaving the teacher in complete confusion when they wanted to show an educational film.

I loved those stories. They made me remember that teachers are vulnerable human beings, too, and that being a student didn't necessarily mean that one had to be a victim like in my case with Mr. Oxblood.

David had lots of good advice for me in that regard and came up with witty answers or how to react when some chalk would land on my head. He recommended engaging Mr. Oxblood in pointless debates that had a double meaning. David loved these endless disputes with the authorities, but he, in comparison to myself, was liked and respected FOR that. But anyways, his advice to add some hidden, devious humor that only classmates were able to understand, worked. Now the jokes were on him.

Now that the class started to laugh about Mr. Oxblood instead of me, I felt a bit more empowered, but let me tell you, it didn't make me want to go to his classes more often nor gave me better grades. That case was lost. I had let go. I would get through. I was not alone anymore. I had a friend now. David and I were carved out of the same type of wood. I admired him. I had found a new, male, and well-respected ally, and my confidence experienced some kind of a renaissance. I thought of him as my mentor and soon, the best friend I ever had - even more than that. One day, it took me by complete surprise, and I realized that I must be, undoubtedly, IN LOVE.

Yayyy!!! Um… I mean, oh no. Bummer, actually. Let me stop this love train right here with a big hair-raising "screeeeeech." I'd like to do the situation justice from here. Please allow me to take off the rose-red glasses of first head-over-heels teenager Liebe.

Let me explain to you who David was from the perspective I have today. As lovely and funny as he was back then, he also was a bit of a bully, and he and I, spoiler alert, won't embark on a romantic journey from here.

David was what you could call a master manipulator. He knew the tricks in the book about how to utilize power to control others. However, David is still one of my oldest friends, who still has a treasured place in my life. I couldn't imagine that the bond that our past had woven will ever be ripped or cut, despite the hurtful experiences. Let's take a little plunge into those.

While I had gotten close to my new best friend David, my friendship with Cindy suffered even more than before. The troubles with her mom that no one, including me, knew about, paired with her disinterest in my problems, had caused us to grow apart dramatically. The continuing development of different interests and tastes in music, clothes, books, and other people also played a role. Instead, I had David to fill this empty spot.

The situation in regards to the freshly discovered butterflies in my stomach caused by the mere thought of David started to turn into sheer agony. We spent almost every day together. I now also used to hang out at David's place after school for lunch, instead of going home.

Hanging out with David was much better than fighting with my mum, who suspected me now every day of skipping another class. At home, my school antics were a constant theme and turned eating together into a battle of passive-aggressive, low-pitch, lashing-out, and an eye-roll party. After having lunch at David's, we would sit in his room, play with his little sister or Herman the budgie, and talk about school and neighborhood gossip. I hoped the hours would stretch a little so that I could stay longer.

David was sometimes so tired that he asked me if I would mind if he would lay down, and suddenly he would fall asleep in between sentences, as I sat next to him. Did he want me to join him and nap, too, or was this his way of telling me that I had overstayed my welcome?

I never dared to ask, and so I always wrote him amusing little notes and left silently with those butterflies in my tummy that had grown to the size of small airplanes by now, carrying me home on their wings.

The day came when I couldn't find sleep anymore. All I could think of was DAVID! But I foresaw trouble: If it wouldn't work out between the two of us, I would never be able to endure a: the pain of a broken heart in that magnitude and b: the shame of being 'a stupid and silly girl, who just couldn't figure out if a boy liked her or not. I couldn't tell anyone because I didn't want witnesses if I would fail.

For me, being watched by others as I was hurting was a way more humiliating experience as being just me and myself. I had learned that in class. It had bothered me more how the whole class had silently witnessed me becoming someone's doormat than me being alone with my pain. It was a matter of being in control. Suddenly, it clicked, and the solution to move ahead with my heart-troubles was obvious: I had to be brave. I needed to talk to him, take his hand and ask him if he liked me more than a pal, if he wanted me as much as I wanted him. This act of bravery needed some prep-time, but it was doable. I was shy, but at the same time, I wasn't a coward.

After a few days of boosting all the confidence in myself, in David and a positive outcome of "the talk," I decided that the time had come to create opportunities for it. To prepare myself mentally, I went on long walks to practice what I would say, how I would say it, and when.

While restlessly browsing through the neighborhood, I was desperately searching for inspiration on how on earth I could convey to him how I felt without bursting out in laughter or peeing in my pants.

One of those strolls with myself led me to a place where he used to take me for fishing. Going fishing with him at this spot had been one of the most fun days in my memory: there was a little hidden bridge that only a few people knew of, right in the middle of the old town.

At this spot, a stream of water bubbled under an old house into a romantic little river. David was the fisher king of the area and a real expert. On that particular day, we had been fishing there for eels – I thought of this place as "our secret little romantic waterfall." So, on that day, David had caught eight or nine eels, and we had a blast when they swung their long snake-like bodies around the fishing rods, sputtering their slimy fluids mixed with water all over our clothes before they'd land up in a bucket. David had given me a rod as well, and to both of our surprise, I made the most excellent catch of the day: A golden carp.

There is a fairy tale where a girl catches a golden carp, and her wishes come true. David called me his fisher princess and told everyone about my fantastic trophy fish that, in the end, would land in the cathedral pond. Not only that, that poor old carp would also make some headlines in the newspaper as the curiosity of the day. David bragged with that stunt for days and cut out the newspaper article. I felt proud. Sorry, dear golden carp, I should have thrown you back in the river, and I hope your soul can forgive me that your life as a fish ended there in that unlivable chlorine soup.

Anyways, let me reel this bit of the story back in to make sense: there, as I arrived at "our" spot, the little waterfall where we went fishing now and then, and where I had caught a golden carp, I couldn't believe my eyes. Someone had spray-painted an A+D on the wall!

I broke out in a cold sweat. Who had found out what was up with me? Was my cover blown? Someone knew I was in love with David. But who? Or belonged these initials to someone else, maybe Arthur and Doris, Alex and Daniela, Amy and Dan? I hoped so!!!

On the other hand, why would exactly here, at our secret hideaway, right now as I was in the process of gathering all my strength to declare my love for David to David, why would this graffiti appear right this moment in time? The timing and location were just too random and distinct. Had David himself maybe sprayed it there? Feelings of hope started to come back to me. Maybe David had put it there to send me a secret message? Perhaps he was just as helpless in expressing his feelings towards me as I was? I decided right there and then that today was the day, and this graffiti was my sign. Whatever it meant and whoever put it there. I decided that by the end of the day, I would finally know. Honesty was needed urgently.

I walked over to David's place and rang the strange doorbell he had recently put in with the sole intention to make his guests laugh upon arrival, and, of course, to make his mother roll her eyes. It was a sound somewhat between a donkey's fart and a cuckoo clock. His mother opened and, indeed, first rolled her eyes, but then we broke out in laughter together because of that terrible new sound that just wouldn't want to stop. After we caught our breaths, she told me that David was out and about and asked if I wanted to wait inside. I happily agreed because I was afraid that I would change my mind if I'd left.

An hour passed, and I went to his room and waited. Then I went down again to his little sister and watched a bit of TV while she was singing to all the jingles - no sign of David. Nervousness crept in, and so I told his mom that I wanted to wait outside on the steps. I sat down on the warm terracotta tiles that the perfect summer weather in the little town had warmed up. I closed my eyes and bathed my face and naked skin on my arms and legs in this divine and comforting blanket of the gentle, yet profoundly penetrating light. Now and then, a white little fluffy cloud would pass by, a day like a golden kiss to the earth.

I instantly calmed down and felt reassured and almost in a state of silent bliss for a moment right there, under this stunningly clear, blue sky.

After a few minutes of this almost dreamlike state, I opened my eyes again and stared into the open space of the old fish market right in front of me. I had a feeling that David was close now.

The asphalt was steaming, and the hot air played tricks on my vision: It looked like a Fata Morgana when I spotted a person dressed from head to toe in white.

It was David. He looked like an Arabian prince that day, stepping into my direction as if he was coming out of a bizarre and beautiful dream.

But something wasn't right. Something didn't belong there; something was about to pop and to unravel the cheek-smacking truth: He had a companion with him, and this companion, to my utter surprise, was Cindy.

As my stomach started to turn around, a thousand questions exploded in my head at once. When did THEY become friends? When did he meet HER? When did they even spend time together without me knowing about it? Why has none of them ever told me anything about them being friends? Was today the first time they hung out together? He came closer, and Cindy waved. I waved back. They asked me if I wanted to join them for a stroll down to the boathouse.

I agreed, under shock, not knowing, not wanting to see why this day had suddenly taken a completely different turn. We chatted about some meaningless topics. I purposely fell behind for a moment, pretending to take a breather. But what I wanted to do was to look at them to confirm a suspicion I had – indeed, they were holding hands. My only thought was that I so desperately wanted to take his other hand. I didn't want to see the truth and tried to find excuses for them, walking around holding hands. I pleaded with myself internally for a few depressing minutes: "Maybe this is only a symbol of friendship for them?" It wasn't.

And Cut!

If my friendship with Cindy had been rocky before, this was the immediate and irreversible death of it. Silently, discreetly. I was heart-broken.

I spent the next few days crying and being angry with myself about how stupid I had been. What could I do now? Why didn't David know that WE were supposed to be together, not him and Cindy? I mean, I had liked Cindy, too, until that day at least, but in my eyes, Cindy was one of those girly-girls, trying to unconditionally please with laced underwear, purple bikinis, and painted toe-nails and stuff like that. He should know and pick better than that! I thought that what he and I had, the pranks, the fishing, the back-talking, and the dirty jokes, was worth so much more!

It was just plain stupid. According to what I just had experienced, this so-called "love," if it existed beyond pro-creation, was only pain and a dangerous game. The whole deal with friendships was similar: a total farce. I concluded that people are animals, only watching out for themselves, trying to survive, trying to beat others, if not eat them. I would NOT allow myself to feel like this again and closed my heart carefully and tightly. No one would ever be allowed to have access to me in this way. Never again would I lose control of myself in this way and make myself a vulnerable, whimpering victim of others. I concluded that one had to be smart and in control to get ahead in life, and ridicule what one couldn't have.

My broken heart over David was a lousy advisor. I came up with a strategy: instead of cutting him out as a friend as I had done it with Cindy, I chose to become an even "better" friend to David than I had been before. "Let's wait it out and see what time will do to their blossoming relationship," is what I thought to myself, hoping for David's love-bubble to burst as soon as it had appeared. I would be more than happy to provide the needles to prick it. What once was sacred and blissful between David and me was now a bitter sting in my chest. A bite of jealousy and evil wishes for both of them.

Their relationship, which I considered to be a fluke, was not just made out of soap and water but seemed to consist of glue and cement. Their romantic involvement would continue to exist for eight more years. How much time of pointless, bitter, and silent wait it would cost me. If the disorder-level of my life until then would compare to the size of a flowerpot for bulimia to grow in, it now had turned into a commercially sized hot-house.

I bottled up so much, including my severe problems at school, that I soon wouldn't know where to offload it all anymore. I had run out of options. There was no one left to be honest with. I believed that I had driven everyone away and found myself in complete isolation. Wearing the mask of friendship for David, while trying to sabotage his relationship had perfected my two-faced existence. So much, that I almost lost sight of what was and wasn't real.

I radically and violently suffocated my feelings to be able to stay close to David without breaking down because of the inner pain that I suppressed. I learned to ignore my genuine emotions with all my might. Instead, I realized that if I began to nourish feelings of despise for others in my heart, especially for Cindy, the "stupid cow", and all of these other stupid people at school, teachers included, I felt strong.

Seen from today's perspective, I stepped on a path of imagined superiority and self-righteousness to make the inner agony go away because I felt like a prisoner. I can relate to how narcissism starts. And how broken people feel inside that have no kindness for others left and need to manipulate to feel in control.

OF COURSE, none of my problems were Cindy's fault. It wasn't as if she had crossed me behind my back or something like that. I hadn't told her about my feelings and had been very good at hiding them. Many years later, David said to me that when we all first met at the boat-house, back then over 25 years ago, he was mesmerized by me but went for Cindy because she had simply "made it easier" for him to kiss. That was all. She had made it less complicated.

If I could have only looked in the future, instead of anger, I would have felt compassion and empathy for them because their path would not lead them to a "happily ever after"-ending...

During their eight years together as a couple, Cindy's mother and Cindy herself would have to endure severe mental health issues. The relationship that David had chosen because he thought it was "easier" would turn out to be a huge emotional burden on both, changing him drastically in many ways. I was sure that they would marry one day, but over the years, their co-dependency turned into a dark and difficult journey. Today, I like to believe that David saved Cindy's life by loving her and making her laugh and that she saved his life in return, by making him a sensitive and caring man and partner, instead of the loud-mouthed bully he once used to be.

When I bumped into Cindy about ten years ago in the little town with the cafes on the cobbled streets and the old cathedral, we had nothing but kind words for each other. Bless you, Cindy. I hope you have found happiness and fulfillment.

Back in the past, a few months after my heart-break over David and close to the end of the school year, I remember sitting in my room, thinking: "What could I do today… hmmm… what about my first joint?".

I called David and asked him if he could help me out. He surely wouldn't bring Cindy along to that. She was anti-drugs. I was right - what a perfect opportunity to come up with something that could be our little secret. I took devious pleasure in pulling strings like a puppet master. That feeling in itself alone was worth trying to smoke pot for.

David arranged the necessary and invited me as usual to his place. He took me by my hand, great start, led me up the stairs, opened the door to the attic. He got a ladder, we climbed upstairs, up, up, up, and a few minutes later, we sat on a little table where he showed me how to roll a joint.

I tried it, and it turned out perfectly slim, and my skills were appreciated ever since. We smoked it, went to a café, and sat there for a solid two hours without saying a word. Suddenly David looked at me, laughed, and told me that he had been talking to me in his head for all that time. He explained that he had imagined a whole conversation with me. Asking me questions and hearing my imaginary answers to it and so forth. How much fun THAT was, uh-huh… But I was thrilled. This new drug was great to have as a secret, our little thing that we did behind Cindy's back. I loved it. The plan had worked.

Marijuana was a perfect addition to my activities outside of school (while there was school). It made the time when I was skipping math classes go by so much faster, and I also felt I had a lot of fabulously creative ideas when I was high. The best effect it had, however, was that I didn't feel guilty anymore when I sat there, somewhere outside with my notebook while the other "idiots" were at school.

I now had started to dread school altogether, not just math lessons. I severed that part and environment from the person I had become: a drug-using misunderstood rebel against the theft of my human dignity, left to my own devices. I now considered my classmates as "children" who did as the teacher told them. They were incapable of even second-guessing their actions (or lack thereof) and, for that reason, dependent weaklings.

 The thought of being packed in a room together with those pimply conformists was ridiculous. YUK! In my self-created world that ticked according to my own rules now, no one could hurt me anymore. I became a runaway from my insecurities and my wounded little teenager's heart.

What the hell was I thinking? What was I looking for? I guess the answer comes in three simple words: Respect, acceptance, and love.

But can one summarize the human desires to these three simple points? What would you add? What are you looking for in your life if you boil it down? Can we get what we need by denying who we are, as I did?

If we do not allow our true feelings to emerge, but inste it means that we have to embark on a journey that demands significant efforts in terms of keeping up with a growing net of It's a rat race with yourself, leading to nothing good.

OMING A BULLY

~ Further Left… ~

...ce David and Cindy were hanging out more and more until they were together ALL the time and smoking pot was not the binding glue I had hoped it would be, I got a little prickly towards David.

I also didn't like going to the rowing club that often anymore, because of these two slobber-faces. Both of them had spoiled that former happy-place in my life, the rowing-club, too. They were all over each other all the time, kissing, fumbling, giggling. It was everything that I wanted myself but didn't get - right in front of my eyes, as soon as I stepped out of the dressing room. To distract myself, I started to flirt with one of the other guys, who was in David's team. Of course, I flirted very obviously in front of David, but my heart was still aching over him. I wanted to hurt him, and he should get the clear message that he wasn't the number one guy in my life anymore.

More and more often, I tried to use David as a target for a joke or prank. But oh boy, I had picked the wrong person to play this game with.

Challenging David made him upset, and he started to avoid me and gave me disrespectful nick-names – one of them, the worst, was "Ficknudel," aka "Fuck-noodle." I am laughing out loud, as I am writing this memory down - How I had dreaded that name! He was good at getting under my skin - in the best and worst way.

Despite my knowledge that David was the wrong person to mess with, I kept on provoking him because I was MAD AT HIM and couldn't maintain my anger. It was a lost battle, and he began to shoot back with even meaner jokes and remarks. He was better at this than me.

A month in, the name-calling and joking about me got to me so much, I made a pact with myself: From now on, I would never be a bully victim - EVER - again. I would rather die hitting back than giving in and showing a single tear to anyone. I remember that I was boiling inside, ready to explode at all times, thinking about how to get back in control, and there came my perfect opportunity: Vera.

I met Vera at church. Yes, church, that's right. Despite being an atheist, there was no way around going to church. It was part of going to school. So, one morning, sitting in the choir, this big girl was sitting next to me. She sang so whole-heartedly off-key that I had to crack up in the middle of the Kyrie!

She had no clue why I was laughing, and so she joined in. I remember my thoughts:" O my God, what an incredibly stupid and naïve chick… I think I am going to make her my friend because she is SO ridiculous that she will distract from anyone targeting me. This girl is hard to miss." I planned it this way, and I cold-bloodedly executed it - my first false friendship.

With Vera, there was always a good laugh going on. Unnoticed by her, most of the time, I laughed about her, not with her, though. Her presence in my life was refreshing, yes, no doubt, but her "usefulness" was weighing in much more than her potential as a real friend. People started to ask me questions about her because they found our sudden friendship very oddly matched. I, behind her back and to my devious pleasure, enjoyed answering those questions and spiced them with harmful, private, and embarrassing stories she had told me confidentially. I called her "my project" or "my social study case."

Being a bully and a snitch started to become addictive, fast. I felt power. The very same power that enables bullies to believe that they are invincible, and I was now one of them! And nothing would stop me.

I asked Vera to join the rowing group. She was unsuitable for rowing, but I most definitely would use her to make everyone laugh about her. My plan had worked. Soon, Vera became the target for everyone's subtle jokes. Slowly, I regained respect for being ruthless at the rowing club.

The girls on my team happily giggled along with me in the changing rooms while I was making faces behind Vera's back. To the boys, I would point out how the end of the boat, where Vera was sitting, would sink deeply into the water - what a blast. Ha, Ha.

In the end, I even got my friendship with David back on track – also thanks to pulling off that mean stunt with Vera.

Vera was unassuming and trusted me blindly. She was so grateful for having me in her life. What a perfect victim. On a side note (let me be clear), these are the most horrible things one could do to someone, and I still feel terrible about this today. But I know she is doing well today, and probably the happiest, most beautiful, and grounded person I know.

I don't know how I did it, but I brainwashed Vera into believing she was in love with David, and I told her that I knew that David was in love with her as well. She didn't believe me that there was a chance that David would possibly requite her passion, but I made up a ridiculous story of how David had confided in me.

I added that the relationship with Cindy was on the rocks anyway. I went all out in my devilish fairytale and described in detail all those things that David had supposedly said: that all he wanted and needed was a "real woman" as a girlfriend, someone who also might be more sexually daring than Cindy. When I used the word "sexually," Vera blushed and giggled. She was falling for it.

I suggested that Vera should write a love letter and that I would happily assist her in making sure she would hit the "right tone." She agreed, of course - the poor thing. Listening to my evil instructions, she composed the most bizarre love-letter that the world has ever seen.

Its content sounded as if it was written by three-year-old tripping on magic mushrooms. I was good at convincing people.

The bolder the lies, the easier this game seemed to work. By assuring Vera that David had a brilliant sense of humor and that he was also a little pervert, was enough reason for Vera to put her name under this incredibly moronic letter. It contained perverted poetry and drawings of dancing sperm cells. We both licked the envelope to seal it, and she looked at me with such hopeful and excited eyes. I promised her prompt and personal hand-delivery.

As soon as she left my house, I wandered down the cobblestoned alley that would lead me to David's house. My heart was pounding. I hadn't seen him in his home for a while. It was around 8 pm and dark outside, but I was in luck: he was at home and opened the door.

It was the first time after this long and estranged period that I was standing here again on his doorstep, listening to the ridiculous ring of his doorbell, enhancing the awkwardness of the moment. Not too long ago, these steps had been my favorite place in the world.

To my surprise, David reacted very positively to seeing me. He smiled, cracked a joke, and asked me to come in. When I gave David the letter, he looked astonished. I told him to read it out loud. First, he was in utter disbelief that something like this could be real, but after a few seconds, he almost peed himself because of all the laughter to follow.

We were laughing so hard, loud and long, like in the good old days. I felt that I had my friend back. My plan had paid off. After this prank on Vera, all went back to almost normal - for everyone, but Vera.

After accepting my lies like a trooper when I told her that David was "not ready" for another relationship and that he was trying to work it out with Cindy, she fell in love with someone else… and she did something with the guy that I was far from doing with ANYONE - she had SEX!

After making me promise that I would never tell anyone, yeah, right, she let me in on every little detail of how she had slept with that someone. Wow. I was jealous as hell but would have never admitted it.

Vera had met the guy during a volunteer job in a summer camp, where she looked after little kids in the forest. Losing her virginity was a sacred moment for her. Still, for me, her most intimate confession was only a great new opportunity to release my feelings of anger against the world, that I had bottled up. Causing harm to others, felt strangely good, and gaining popularity by making people laugh felt even better. Without realizing, I had finally learned something from my math teacher - what a brilliant new scandal and rumor to spread that I could put to use for my purposes.

I pulled as many details out of Vera as I could. She told me that the guy "initially couldn't find his way in" until she whispered in his ear:" further left." I made sure that "further left" would become the new secret code that not just the rowing club, but the whole school would know about. Everyone was in stitches about this poor girl's most private experience that she had shared with me, heart to heart.

But I loved my ill-intended games and drew energy from it like a vampire. It had gotten to the core of my being, and along with becoming a real asshole, I had become a compulsive liar. Because lying felt like pure magic! To lie about everything could make me look perfect in an instant! I sometimes would listen to myself while I was talking to someone and think "Wow… where does this shit come from? This is nuts. Well, if people believe this nonsense, then it's their own fault."

After a while, playing my terrible games with Vera and others became less and less appealing. Feelings of guilt and depression kicked in because of what I was doing to Vera behind her back. Crap. How did that happen?

Oh no. There were downsides to this new me. Most annoyingly, a side effect of spending so much time together, I even accidentally had started to like Vera. The sad truth is that I had no other friends, due to keeping everyone miles away from my true self. Thanks to my lies and their fear of me. Just like in math, no one wanted to be the next victim. One sleepless night it dawned on me - I had stepped on the path where nothing I would ever do could be right.

I knew that I had become addicted to these power-games and lies. My bullying and falseness had taken over, and the toxic momentum it had amassed had become an all-consuming avalanche. That night, I knew that I had to come clean.

Alexander the Great came to my mind, and the Gordian knot he had cut with his sword instead of detangling it. Instantly, I realized that there was only one solution to this complex and horrible behavior that I had allowed into my life. The only way to save myself from becoming a real bad egg was to set a radical end to this, and the one thing I could do instantly was to start right away with being honest again.

The next time that we went rowing at the clubhouse, I told Vera that I wanted to share the rowing boat for two that Cindy and I always used to row when we trained together. Vera agreed happily, and we rowed out in silence. After 20 minutes, I gently stopped the boat with my sculls, and we slowly came to a halt in the far end corner of the canal, where no one would see or hear us.

Vera looked exhausted and didn't have the slightest clue about what was about to happen next. She was behind me, and I couldn't, and I also didn't want to see her face, so I turned myself halfway around and took a deep breath. After a moment, I opened the conversation, stating that I had to tell her something. "Vera," I said, "It's all a lie. I was never your true friend. I used you and talked badly about you behind your back. Pretty much the whole time from when we met to now. I gave away your secrets and made jokes about you so that the others would like me more. The fact is, I realized that I like you and that you are a great girl and I think this has to end. I am sorry."

Vera stayed silent. She didn't reply at all, but I felt the boat jiggle a little bit after a while of awkward silence. Vera was desperate that I wouldn't hear her cry. She didn't make a peep all the way home. We finally rowed back, still in utter silence, and that was the end of our false friendship, and all other ship- or boat rides together because she quit rowing, and we never really spoke again. But it was also, thank GOD, the end of me being a bully as well.

From then on, I was radically honest. That worked for a little while as a new approach, at least when it came to others, but not when it came to myself. I confused being honest with myself with being my own worst critic, spotlighting only the negative and dark within me. When I was honest with myself in that fashion, I told myself over and over how useless, ugly, evil, and hated I was. I simply couldn't forgive myself for what I had done.

I unconsciously began to practice another detrimental toxic habit, another key ingredient for getting an eating disorder: the endless, self-critical, and dismissive inner monologue. This whole exercise had taught me a valuable lesson that would become a key lesson of my disease AND healing since it goes both ways.

If I start something small, it grows and eventually ends big. I wished that I had been aware of this lesson that I learned with Vera when I made my first experiences with a little binge here and a little harmless purge there. "This is just for diet reasons. Everyone is doing it, right?"

I wished I would have known the difference between honesty and self-abuse, but the contrary was the case.

FIRST BOYFRIEND, FIRST BULIMIC THOUGHTS

~ I Should have Picked the Frying Pan ~

Mile-marker. Having done the worst, as in becoming a bully and stopping myself from staying in this utterly dark realm, is a significant step in recovery.

Coming clean with the ones we hurt, is embarrassing but incredibly helpful. You gain a piece of dignity back. From there onward, the repair we start within our environments slowly enters our inner realm and affects how we treat ourselves. But it takes time.

I see my time as a bully as the worst of all times. Yet again, I am grateful, because it taught me the pattern that I like to call "The Chain of Pain," where hurt received from others, is being passed on to the next best weaker person. I use this term to explain to my kids why one tries to hurt the other after being disciplined for something by a parent. This understanding helped my kids to stop their unconscious behavior, and the problem has almost vanished. They know they can use better tools than throwing their sibling under the bus. Isn't it fascinating to see that even little ones can practice self-efficacy if given a chance to understand that a pattern is going on?

Allowing myself to experience this low level was also a significant key in forgiving my abusers. I know that someone has hurt them to be like that. That doesn't mean I have to be their doormat, but it helps me to remove myself from their reach without having to harbor anger towards them, which ultimately hurts me - not them.

If that was the most shameful episode, one of the most humbling points in my life was approaching: I had to repeat a year because I had missed 256 hours of class at school. What? Do you wonder how I didn't see that coming? Me, too. I am still scratching my head! God only knows how I had managed to get away with false and self-written excuses in the name of my mom up until then. Utter delusion, I guess.

In my confused, lonely, and depressed headspace, I had clung onto the belief that my grades all over were still good enough to get me through this year. I didn't expect the teachers to get serious. But they did and had made up their minds to let me feel the consequences of my behavior.

Neatly plotted out, they all dropped my balancing grades one down for the sole purpose of me failing to reach the number of points that I needed. I was horrified! A YEAR LONGER with these immature and stupid cowards - now with even younger and more stupid people! O, MY GOD!!!

My parents were shocked - mortified. So was I. This was the end of the world. I shaved my head in response to that. My father met me on the street after I visited the hairdresser, sporting my 2mm result. He didn't recognize me at first, but after a second, his jaw dropped, and he realized who I was. He turned away, took out his wallet, and tore a little black and white picture of me into tiny, sad squares that sailed down silently on the cobbled street in our small and peaceful town. I caught a glimpse of his red and watery eyes when I grabbed his arm. He turned away and just walked. I kept standing there for a while and didn't understand what was wrong with him.

The new, supposedly liberating cut only felt great for about a week, and then it turned into a sob fest. Weighing in these tears made the whole coolness factor not worth the while. I cried many nights over missing my long hair and wanting to be looking like a girl again.

On top of wanting my long hair back, I discovered the unexpectedly ugly shape of the back of my head - it was flat like a pancake! Oy vey, there it was, yet another imperfection. I felt horrible in my own skin. I, as you already have figured out, wasn't one of the straight-forward, mainstream beauties, the Cindy-girls everybody wanted.

Neither was I a cool, tomboyish girl in biker boots and Vespas (little scooters that everyone who was hip used to scoot around with). I wasn't one of those girls that wore a bikini at the pool. Let me remind you, I was one of those girls where the belly button was a deep hole surrounded by a doughnut of fat that I saw when I looked at my own mid-section.

I acted as if I was confident, but I started to stare hours and hours in the mirror that just wouldn't want to change the picture. Everything was wrong with me now, and that stupid hairstyle was about to grow out, which made me look even worse! Really, it DOES look silly if you let your hair just grow after cutting it back to 2mm, can you imagine?

I tried to fix my hair by putting a ton of styling products in it. Some hair spray smells can still make me cry when I catch a whiff of them today; their scents send me back in time, and I can feel the old pains of that time, too. Thank God, yet again, that life moves on!

This phase was a tough one - and don't get me started on my non-existent love life. Everyone had a boyfriend or girlfriend, or at least a love-interest. Even my brother! Her name was Reena, a redhead with a model body. Her belly was so flat that she looked like a surfboard, but yet she had booooooobs - adorable.

Reena's classmate and also best friend was one of those cool tom-boy Vespa chicks that I secretly admired. She had a popular and handsome boyfriend who played the guitar in a band. Like Reena, she had a similarly fantastic body. I was jealous that I wasn't a dream girl, like those two - no love for me. I had gathered a bit of kissing and petting experience, but once something happened with a guy, people either ran away from me the next day or behaved as if nothing had ever happened, and I didn't know what to do.

When I think back, I know that I was the problem, not them, playing the "I-am-so-mature-I-do-not-care-game." Why? The only answer I have today is that my motives originated in utter confusion, suppressed anger, and the fear of getting hurt. I can find so many reasons for the chronic pain-level I was in. I thought that my parents, for example, had given up on me.

I felt that nothing in this world made sense anymore. I tried to remember my perfect angel self from when I was younger, but all I could see was a stupid girl.

Now I was grown-up and had transformed into an ugly, useless, and sometimes even evil slob. I was also smoking cigarettes, despite the fact that I had detested smoking as a child.

I also started to abuse alcohol, instead of just drinking a little here and there like the other kids my age. In Germany, the legal age to drink is 16, but kids start even earlier than that. My decline was fast, and at age 15, I drank for the sole purpose of getting wasted. I drowned my feelings of having failed my perceived foolishness due to what had happened at school. I had underestimated what it meant to mess with authority.

I ate the whole humble-pie I got served, without leaving a crumb on the plate. Defeated, I threw my hands in the air and stepped into the role of the sad clown and loser that life seemed to have reserved for me - with a pathetic hairstyle to match. Looking at all this, I was a hot, raw mess and not ready for any kind of relationship.

One afternoon, my brother and I were playing Rainbow Island on our old PC Schneider, a computer game where you had to run around in a castle to jump over little cakes and biscuits, ice cream, and cookies. Every time one jumped, one would leave a rainbow behind. After scoring a bunch of them, my brother told me in a side sentence that he was wondering if he should break up with Reena. I asked him why, and he vaguely replied that he thought she was crazy. Hypnotized by the game, I asked him, only half interested, why he thought she was crazy, and he replied, drumroll, here it comes: that she would make herself throw up to stay thin.

I couldn't believe what I just heard and stopped playing my game - what she was doing sounded so bizarre to me! I had only heard about purging from the old Roman emperors who did that when they had an orgy, and my response was absolutely inappropriate - I had to laugh out loud! Simon thought I didn't take him seriously, and he added "no, no, they are crazy, I am not making this up - her friend is doing it, too. HER FRIEND SAYS: WHO DOESN'T DO IT IS STUPID. They think this is funny, you know? I think it is totally mad."

After recovering from my laughter, I changed my mind about this in an instant: not only was this NOT FUNNY. This was OUTRAGEOUS! UNFAIR! THAT was why they looked so good! THAT was the secret of being a dream girl! I was furious. I felt personally insulted by them because they indirectly had called me stupid, too! Because it had never occurred to me that this was the way and means of getting the perfect body. This moment was the first time I HEARD about bulimia.

Only a month away before my finger would find its way down MY mouth, I met Stefan. Phew! The devil must have sat on my shoulder, but as I told you before, I now have no regrets, not even Stefan. I was busy with having landed a part in a play at my school and another role in another school's theatre group. People from that school had seen me in a show and asked me to help them out because one of the actresses had dropped out. She felt the part was "too small" for her. I was intrigued by that part and gladly accepted.

I was one of three "Erynnies," a creature from hell, a Goddess of revenge and punishment. I loved this role, even if it was relatively small, compared to the more substantial parts, I would typically get. But with this one, I felt I could pour out what was inside of me - my anger and suppressed energy. We crawled on the floor, howled, scratched, and let our tongues dangle out of our mouths, and honestly did a fantastic job with these roles.

During one of the performance nights, there was a sudden wave of excitement backstage "Stefan is coming tonight! Oh my God, STEFAN is coming tonight!" Who the f*** was Stefan? I disliked him already because of the effect he had on others. I found out that this Stefan-guy had been accepted into a fairly prestigious drama school. In Germany, it is hard to get into one of these conservatories. Stefan, a former student of the school that put up the play, had now "moved on to doing greater and bigger things." Good for him. This guy is a small-town celebrity – Woopdeedoo," is what I thought.

At the time when I met him, he was twenty-six years old, ten years older than I was. Our first personal encounter would happen at the "Knockout," a club that all performers of the show went to for drinks and dancing after the show. I was standing in a dark corner, drenched in blue light, sipping on my Weinschorle, the choice of alcoholic beverage that everyone where I come from drinks to get wasted. Usually, Weinschorle is served in a pint filled with three-quarters of white wine and one-quarter of sparkling water. In my circle of friends, we would drink about four to seven each night. That sometimes makes about two and a half bottles of wine per head – ouch! Slightly drunk like that, I would usually watch the people dance, and pick out boys that I would later try to hook up with. Standing there in my corner, busy with my first schorle, I suddenly, as if magic powers were working on me, had to turn my head around to see this person entering the room.

The being was standing on top of a steep flight of stairs, leading down to the dance-floor. The guy with those long blond curls that I stared at, literally bathed in the whitish-yellow spotlight pointing straight down on him, making these fantastic golden curls extra shiny. I thought "This MUST be that Stefan-dude. Look at how he is presenting himself on those stairs. Who does he think he is?? Brad Pitt? What a prick, what an arrogant a$%-hole!"

I instantly knew, even if I had never met him before, that this was the guy everyone had gushed about, and yes, I hated him already, but I was also fascinated. My inner dialogue continued "Well, let's wait and see if there is a possibility to play a little game with him." He came across as the archetype of a picture-perfect self-obsessed, vain, knob-head. The way he moved was so utterly pathetic and overly theatrical to me. His chest was sticking out, swollen up with pride like a rooster, and brimming with blown up self-importance. With every inch of his body language, he screamed silently into the world "Look at me! I am valuable, amazing, and sooooooo well trained!' - "OMG – he is artificial as f#$%!" were word snippets that flashed through my mind.

I observed him as he started a conversation with someone. I noticed that he was scanning the room. He was looking for chick-prey. His outwardly performed, big, ridiculously larger-than-life gestures accompanied his every thought - what a faker.

And just as if it was scripted in a movie, he walked up to me, or better, he finally let himself glide down from his cloud of self-enjoyment, blessing me with his attention. My blood was boiling because of this immediate, intense dislike I felt for this guy, but I pretended to be a nice, naïve girl. I thought to myself: "Well, let him speak for a while before you smash him with a verbal frying pan over his curly head."

"You were great," he opened the conversation. What did he just say? Wait. What? I was taken aback. Instead of starting a bitching party, I, to my own surprise, felt my inner hostility deflate in an instant, and I observed myself helplessly melting like a marshmallow in a cup of hot cocoa. Darn. I couldn't help it, but I felt flattered. Ego is a powerful thing, what can I say.

We sat down, had some red wine, and talked about theatre and his brother, who was a tantra therapist. I didn't have a clue what that was all about - Indian cooking to music? He also gave me detailed professional feedback on my performance. He kept on saying how "physical" I was and what dangerous energy I had. Now I felt flattered even more than before. Three glasses of red wine later, mixed with the schorle I had already consumed, he shared that his father had recently died and that his mother had lost her marbles over that. My instant disapproval towards him had turned into genuine sympathy. For a split second, I could see his whole life, that whole blown up theatrical spectacle as the direct translation of his sad life. I felt sorry for him. His loud and overly pronounced way of speaking and his artificially blown up self-importance continued, but from that moment on, he was forgiven. We even said good-bye with a hug.

When I came home around three am, I found my father sitting at the kitchen table in his bath-robe. He was reading the newspaper under a dim light with an empty cup and a chamomile tea bag squeezed out, lying there, on a little plate, looking like I was feeling. I walked into my room without a word and dropped into a deep drunk sleep until my mother woke me up with a cold and bitter voice: "School." I got grounded and had no pocket money for a week, but only three days later, I disobeyed and went out after a loud fight with my parents, because they had found cigarettes in my jacket.

Thank God they didn't know anything about my weed stash! I slammed the door, went to the "Knockout," got drunk, and lost myself. Later that night, for the first time, I went to a dance club for older folks in town, called "Force." It looked like a nightclub right out of the eighties, full of blue neon lights and mirrors. This was clearly not the right scene for me. Only the extreme night hawks I knew gathered there after three or four a clock because the "Force" shut its doors on the weekends only around six in the morning when everything else had already closed.

Right then, I preferred being there compared to the other clubs because I could drench my sorrow unseen by the usual crowd.

Yet, I didn't have to be alone with myself. It was a gathering of pathetic drunks with perms, heavy make-up, and horrible clothes, including myself. Leaning against a wall, as usual, I held on tightly to my alcoholic drink, steering towards my favorite relief of being wasted, drenched in the blue, unreal light of the dance floor.

Cutting like a mighty steamship through a wall of fog, Stefan emerged out of a thick curtain of cigarette smoke with his brother. He was the only person there that I knew. It was too loud, so instead of talking to me, he kissed me, marking the start of my first relationship.

A few evenings later, Stefan and I had some sort of "the talk," and he convinced me that we should have an "open relationship," whatever that meant. He explained how this was the best solution for us, because he still lived in Munster, a 2-hour train ride away. He went into detail about what he thought was appropriate: both of us were allowed to "kiss whoever we wanted to" and stay "free human beings." Theoretically, I liked that idea, because my heart was locked tightly anyway, thanks to my David experience. I remember thinking that this set-up was very mature. Little did I know that I had just been recruited as an under-age f^$@-buddy (yikes).

This mature freedom would severely disturb my understanding of loyalty and of having a deep relationship, on top of the gloomy outlook on love that I already had - silly me. I would pay him back later for his lessons on how not to conduct a loving relationship, especially not the first one, with my virginity. The whole "sacred" relation to my hymen was non-existent from the get-go anyway. I was sure that I already destroyed it during a sports accident where I had landed in a weird position after trying to catch a ball.

After going back to Munster for the next two weeks, Stefan came back to town. I decided to venture out on a long walk, and suddenly I thought it would be a great idea to venture all the way to Stefan's mother's house in Durkenbach, a small village just outside the place where I was born. The walk was about an hour or so.

The fields were beautifully dozing in the cold autumn sun. Singing Tom Waits' "It's time, time, time, that you love, well it's time, time, time," I was so far away from understanding what those lines meant. At one point, my walk led me out of nature, and I had to cross a motorway – one obviously never walks to Durkenbach! Was there no other path than the four-lane freeway with these honking vehicles on it? I finally found his mom's house and oddly shaped building surrounded by a small, dreamy pine forest. I knocked on the door.

I can recall my amazement when Stefan opened. He wore a purple-pink-turquoise tracksuit made out of parachute material, Birkenstock sandals, and white tennis socks. They looked like the ones, that German tourists with beer bellies and little khaki hats, are famous for. I tried not to laugh out loud but chuckled instead, stunned by this fashion crime, and followed him into the house. My first impression of the intestines of the "Villa Stefan" was: THIS PLACE IS DARK!

Almost all rooms were carpeted with green oriental rugs EVERYWHERE - on floors as much as on the dark wooden walls. The interior design looked like the old castles that the region in Germany where we come from is so famous for. Knight's armor, ancient weapons, a deer head, and a gigantic dark iron chandelier completed the Game of Thrones look.

His mother, a mousey-type older woman with a small, sharp nose and two big and naive looking eyes, came running after us. Her blonde, short hair was all fluffed up as if she was ready for a High-Tea appointment with the queen of England. His mum reminded me of one of those ladies who go to the hairdresser for washing and blow-drying. She was most undoubtedly lovely, but I was irritated when she told me that she had just baked two (!) cakes. Extra for me.

As she continued to chatter away, she came across as quite confused and anxious. When she stated that the house was bugged with microphones and that people were spying on her on the streets, I wasn't sure how I should reply. Therefore, I didn't respond at all and politely ate cake. Umm, I mean cakes - plural. They were rich and decorated a bit over the top as if baking cakes was the only thing this poor woman was doing all day in her dark castle of loneliness.

After stuffing myself with two massive pieces of buttercream over-load, Stefan took me by my hand and led me down into the cellar, his empire, on the other end of a spiral staircase. This time, I couldn't retain my laughter when I entered his room - this was even worse than his outfit! I felt as if I had walked right back to the '80s and was on the set of Dynasty.

A HUGE wall-filling palm tree scenery perfected the interior design bombardment of lousy taste. His wooden bed in the corner looked like it was a sad remnant from his childhood days in the middle of this overwhelming visual attack.

Stefan lit a candle and stated that he was hungry, yes, even after all that cake. He briefly disappeared up that spiral staircase and came back with a toaster, bread, camembert, and garlic. Magic Stefan turned the toaster on the side, and we grilled the French cheese with the roasted pieces of fresh garlic on top of it. I was already so stuffed, but he told me that it would make him upset if I wouldn't try. It was delicious, and we ended up eating a lot of it. I do not know how I survived the expansion of my stomach muscles that night. After our food orgy, Stefan got us some wine, and after two sips, he carried me to his wooden kiddie bed and started to undress me. In his opinion, it was time to do IT. He made that clear.

I felt so full of all this buttercream, sugar, toast, cheese, and garlic and felt genuinely uncomfortable in my own skin. On top of being an overstuffed sausage filled with ingredients that do not mix very well, I couldn't help cringing at the way he initiated things. It was so obvious, planned out, and predictable like a medical appointment. Was I trapped in an awkward movie or a poorly scripted soft porno? I started laughing again.

Shaking his hands off of me, I told Stefan to go to the bathroom to help himself instead of continuing here with me. I wasn't feeling this contrived way of doing it, especially not for my first time. He backed off and disappeared for about twenty minutes, while I fell asleep. The red wine had done its trick. Looking at the situation today, I, of course, acknowledge how insensitive I have been. But at that moment, I was just trying to be honest. I didn't think of anything wrong. My goodness, he was an adult man, and I was a virgin teenager, he should relax, I thought. Relax and leave me be!

When Stefan came back, he sat down, woke me up, and said that he was upset. He added that he would have kicked me out immediately but acknowledged that I was probably just a little young. I countered that I didn't understand what his problem was. Wasn't honesty the deal between us, even if it would sting?

He looked confused and drove me home. We did it the next day, however, while his Tantra brother was in the room next to us with someone else. It felt like eating a leftover piece of cold cheese with garlic from the day before. Don't get me wrong, it wasn't exactly horrible, but there was no magic. All in all, my first time was utterly unexciting and meaningless. All that hype about the first time, the fear and pain, some girls described, was strange to me. Sex, after this first experience, indeed was a fun sport, but that whole romance/passion thing - no, thank you.

I didn't know the difference between sex and making love. Stefan surely wasn't the best teacher. Sorry, Stefan, you weren't. Three days later, I started the ugly business, that is the subject matter of this book.

FIRST TIME THROWING UP

~ Who doesn't Do It is Stupid ~

Stefan had one more day in town, and we went to watch a movie with Demi Moore and Michael Douglas. Stefan called me "his little Demi Moore" but "with more flesh," and he added that that was "how he liked it."

I didn't like this comparison and evaluation of my body. I felt insulted. In direct and immediate response to his comments about my body, I started a diet and tried to eat thin crispbread and apples all day, nothing else, but that. But to my surprise, two days later, after all this discipline and hunger, I looked even bigger than before! I was bloated, unhappy, and hungry.

There was another problem in addition to my diet failure - I still had to go to Jazz dance twice a week. Home alone, I pondered over having to go to Jazz dance in the evening. I dreaded the thought of schlepping myself there only to watch my bloated self in the mirror, jumping around in a PINK leotard (instead of the white one in ballet) and sweat-pants that squeezed into my waist.

While nibbling on a slice of crispbread in front of the TV, I was desperately trying to make up a reason for not having to go. In addition to my anxious efforts to come up with a good excuse, I was expecting a call from Stefan that just didn't seem to happen. Waiting for his call drove me crazy. He had gone back to Munster a day after sleeping with me, and I hadn't been able to reach him. The first time waiting for a call, you know.

There I was, on a restricted diet, dreading myself and stressing over those issues, home alone, as I allowed myself to get hypnotized by brain-deadening shows on TV. I watched and watched until I concluded that I would NOT be going to my Jazz dance class today. Feeling so weak and bloated, I was the plain opposite of an ethereal being anyway, all because of that stupid diet - enough!

I declared the diet as officially failed and went to the kitchen to have a scratch around and see what kind of food there was. There were a lot of different types of bread - excellent, a good start. I opened the fridge, and a piece of cheese landed in my mouth. I was looking for chocolate, a rare thing in our house.

After I searched several hiding places unsuccessfully, I opened another cupboard and found some chocolate mousse! Excellent! Chocolate spread was even better than chocolate! What a pleasant surprise. I ripped a big chunk from a baguette, grabbed some butter and the glass with the mousse, and went back to the television.

What had started with one piece ended with devouring the whole long loaf of baguette, tons of butter, and almost an entire jar of the chocolate hazelnut spread.

Eating all of it without holding myself back was incredibly soothing and comforting. But once I had finished the binge, I remember looking at the crumbs all over the floor, and right after that, I started to feel sick and disgusted by myself.

As I lay down on the sofa, a massive tummy ache set in. I thought "f%^&ing diet… now I will get even fatter. Fatter and fatter and fatter… doesn't make any difference, does it?" And then… it made a "click" in my brain.

"WHO DOES NOT DO IT IS STUPID!"

Calmly and rationally, I got up, walked to the toilet, and thought, "Well, let's give it a try then." Suddenly, I felt excited, almost as if I was on drugs – what if it would work? What if I would have a body like the desirable girls? What if I would be… THIN and everyone would love me?

It was a fight to bring up the baguette - it was so dry. I had the feeling I was suffocating myself, but then, slowly, slowly everything came up. I felt naughty, relieved, and shortly after very guilty. This trip began unglamorously, with a whole chewed-up baguette and half a jar of chocolate spread staring back at me from the toilet bowl.

If I have had myself as an advisor back then, I would have told myself, that we need to find things that we can emotionally binge on, nourishment that we can keep in, and that fills us! Like self-worth, confidence, trust, reliability and again, and again love for yourself and, therefore, automatically for others. What I would give for a physical magic key that I could just give you right this second. I would love just to put it right here:

....

....

- in between the dotted lines - with a piece of sticky tape. The primary material is the reoccurring mantra of forgiveness, love, gratitude, and the clearing of old traumatic events by making peace with them. Step by step.

It will take a little time to let your forgiveness, love, and gratitude shine onto yourself and the wrongdoers in some of the painful memories of your past, but it will work! Addiction is just a thought pattern that you can resolve because nothing is more potent than forgiveness towards yourself and others. If I would have known how important it is to put myself as number one in my own life.

That I needed first to become my personal best friend, before I could become anyone's friend or partner, that I had to learn to be kind to MYSELF, instead of trying to be 'cool' or in charge, that would have helped.

You cannot be a lover without loving yourself.

AND GOODBYE...

~ Doppelgangers, Cookie-Jars, Fish and Cigarettes ~

About two weeks after my first private food excess with consequences, consequences that I wouldn't have dreamed of in my worst nightmare, I found myself sitting in the train, on my way to Stefan.

A week before, I had taken on the "crisp-bread-and-apple-diet" again, which was difficult because my Grandmother cooked a warm lunch every day and a warm dinner. Both lunch and dinner would always be served warm and were irresistible. I grew up with old school family meals, and it was hard not to develop an appetite because of the inviting smells and flavors wafting through our home.

Initially, I tried to cut back to eating half of the usual meal when I couldn't resist. But because I was still hungry, I binged on the crispbread afterward – and that over the course of a week had led to putting on even more weight.

A day before leaving for Munster, I swore to myself that I would try harder and stopped eating altogether for a day. Monks were able to fast too, so why shouldn't I be able to. I was miserable on the one hand, but on the other, I thought of myself as being disciplined, dieting like that. Trying to starve myself was at least better than doing that "other thing", or running around bloated and gaining weight. So, there I was, sitting in my ICE cabin - feeling hungry and empty. Yet, I felt empowered and disciplined, being able to restrict like that. I tried to use the distraction of this trip to help me with "holding it out" without eating anything.

Wearing a red pair of bellbottom corduroy jeans and a mustard yellow short-sleeve terrycloth polo shirt, I even felt attractive that day. I also had dyed my hair in a new, intense, shiny Henna red that helped me cope with my slight weight gain, as well. I knew how much I put on, to the gram and ounce. During the diet, I had begun to weigh myself about five times a day. Soon this would turn into a 7-year obsession that would happen at least 15-30 times a day. I had promised myself that I would lose the weight (meaning the pound and a half) by not eating at all if I could distract myself enough with the new environment. By the end of this trip, I wanted to be 5 pounds down.

Stefan couldn't pick me up from the train station because he was busy with rehearsals for his final showcase at drama school, but he had described to me how to get to his place. As I sat in one of these little streetcars, pondering upon my life, I suddenly noticed a young gentleman.

He looked a little bit, I kid you not, like an angel, sitting behind a window in the same carriage. Interestingly, the stranger seemed bafflingly similar to Stefan, but the beautiful features were enhanced, and the features I didn't like on Stefan where non-existent. He also had those golden angel curls, but they were even longer and more beautiful. Stefan had a doppelganger, a perfect brother.

I spun this thought further - maybe this twin represented the light, while Stefan represented a kind of sad, selfish, and lost beauty. I needed to look away because my body started aching. I hadn't felt anything like it since David, but this was more intense – HELP!

The station where I had to get out came next. I got up. My heart was beating twice as fast, and I didn't dare to turn around again to look once more. I got off the train. While I tried to fix my suitcase's strap that had become loose, a warm and gentle voice approached me from behind with a friendly "Hi!"

I turned around: it was the beautiful "Stefan-twin." He had a great, sunny smile that washed right over me like a mighty ocean wave - this was a package of bright, pure light. "You are so beautiful - I just had to tell you. Where are you headed?" were the first words to emerge from his very kissable looking lips.

Taken aback, and like in a trance, I told him the name of the street. You know where he lived and wanted to go? The very same street, a few houses further down from where Stefan lived.

We walked together. The handsome stranger was 21 years old and a musician. He carried my suitcase, and I told him about Stefan. He understood that I had a boyfriend but still asked me if I'd like to come for a cup of tea to his place. At that moment, I knew I had a choice. In this case, the right and wrong choice looked like twin brothers.

To me, it was crystal clear that this was a "nice version" of Stefan, a refined version of a man, someone I should be together with. A kind person in whose presence I could feel good about myself. Carefree and uncomplicated happiness had filled me right from the first second after meeting this stranger.

However, I turned his offer of tea down. I almost felt as if I was a little paralyzed, shell-shocked. I couldn't say this simple word: "yes." Instead, I played it cool - my auto-pilot had taken over. Every fiber in me screamed " What are you doing? Why do you let him go without even asking him for his address, number or name?"

We said goodbye in front of Stefan's door. Unbeknownst and thanks to my own efforts of NOT asking, he DID tell me his name before we parted. This is hard to believe, I know, but his name was Stefan as well. Like a shooting star, coming and disappearing into the unknown darkness of time, waving with a soft and sweet smile and wishing me a beautiful day, he went, and I never saw him again.

I was still entranced by my experience with the stranger when I entered Stefan's place. "Whip yourself out of this, Annie," shot through my head, as I had learned with David. While Stefan kissed me, thoughts like "If worse comes to worst, I can just walk around the street, and that other Stefan will find me…" raced through my mind. But of course, I wouldn't walk around the street.

As soon as I had unpacked, Stefan carried me to his bed and wanted to, let me think of a word, "take me," but I turned around and fell in a deep sleep. When I woke up, I found Stefan sitting on the kitchen table over his script, not talking and not looking at me, despite my gentle call. He was pissed. I rolled on my other side and continued my deep, hungry, low-insulin sleep.

The next morning started with breakfast: swiss muesli with forest berries and green bananas. Yellow ones were disgusting in Stefan's eyes. Well, with me, he some sort of had picked a green banana, too. As an extra treat, he gave me a cookie out of a tin, took his bag, and went off to school. He told me that he was going to come back late because he had to meet his friend Renate, a gallery owner. Aha. Who the f^&* was RENATE?

I thought that I should have gone with the stranger on the street! It is so fascinating matter to observe how the brain is capable of recording the original audio track that was going through my mind when I heard the name "Renate" for the first time…

As soon as Stefan was out the door, I finished the whole stash of his treasured cookies that he used to store on his cupboard. Afterward, this time without even giving it further thought, I threw them up. To my surprise, there was no remorse. It was almost a punishment for Stefan too. I had come here to continue my diet and not to be left alone with cookies while he was out with another chick.

When Stefan found me sleeping with the empty cookie tin next to the bed, he got very angry with me. Of course, he didn't know where those cookies had ended up, just eating all of the special treats by myself without leaving him one was bad enough for him.

The week continued awkwardly. There was a lot of sleeping on my side, a lot of rehearsal time on Stefan's, and little sexual activity in between.

At the end of the week, we had dinner at a restaurant. He told me a disgusting story about fish poisoning, and since he was the most overly-expressive actor on the planet, Stefan went into detail "how it felt as if his intestines got sucked out of him." He made these horrible faces of pain and grunted, and I lost my appetite.

I put my plate aside and lit a cigarette. (Yes, back in those days, you could still smoke in restaurants.) I knew that he detested smoking because his father had died of lung cancer, but we were in a restaurant where everyone else smoked cigarettes, and I just had a meal with salmon in it, which he had just ruined for me, so no big deal in my eyes.

He stopped in the middle of one of these fancy facial expressions while mimicking death himself and looked at me, with his eyes bulging out. In a threatening and silent tone, he whispered through his teeth "How dare you?" "...dare what?" I answered. "Smoking in front of me while we are eating?"

I didn't understand his sudden anger right away, because I thought he had finished his meal a while ago. Stefan, instead of eating those last five peas on his plate, had recited his fish-poisoning monologue for about 15 or 20 minutes. But he was furious about the fact that I had lit a cigarette, which was perfectly acceptable if everyone on the table had finished their meals. But he insisted that he hadn't finished. Whatever. After a moment of absorbing is anger towards me, I asked him how HE dared to speak to me like that. And what we both together pretended to have here, a what – a relationship? I concluded my rhetorical question and uttered that I wanted to go home the next morning and that he should better forget about us, and best wishes to Renate anyway.

We didn't speak a single word anymore, and the following day I drove home, still shaking and severely unsettled about why I had allowed myself to get involved with such an old, des-interested guy that I didn't even like.

As soon as I was back home, I immediately started a new diet. This time, I would make sure that I never fail again. I chose to implement purging as an emergency allowance. As soon as I would eat anything that would break my diet, I allowed myself to get rid of it. Finally, something that worked! Having this secret back-up plan, I seemed to be able to stick to the diet much better. Emotionally, however, a problem occurred, that I had not expected. To my own surprise, I missed Stefan.

How did that happen?? How was this possible? I knew I didn't love the guy. I didn't even like him! I didn't realize that this was a little bit like the waning of symptoms one experiences when one gets rid of an unhealthy habit - it was my first breakup.

Wouldn't it be amazing if we could just be switched on with our partnerships from the get-go and only pick what's right for us?

The old saying that friendly people tend to like "a#$%-holes" instead of the nice guy is correct. We often tend to harm ourselves through relationships, and most of us "have to be ready for a nice guy or girl"… isn't that strange? Missing this guy, who I neither respected nor appreciated, made me incredibly angry.

While I lost those desired 5 pounds and with newly gained self-esteem, I threw myself into a few meaningless flings to help me take my mind of Stefan. Thank God that Stefan lived far away!

But as life's humor graces and tests us at the same time, he moved back to town two months later after he graduated from drama school.

Our town was too small, no doubt. Every time I would bump into him, I changed the side of the street until he stopped me one day. "You know, even if it didn't work out with us as a couple, we could work together. I'm planning on directing Miss. Julie (the famous play by Strindberg), and I want you to be in it." I did not see that coming and was very pleased with his suggestion.

When we had our first Miss Julie meeting, he brought along another girl and announced that she was playing Miss. Julie, and that I should play the small part of the kitchen maid. I felt so offended. He had made it sound as if I was supposed to play Miss Julie. I had already memorized the lines! The role of Julie was perfect for me, but instead, he brought in this girl. Was he sleeping with her?

It screamed "ARSEHOLE!!!" in my head, so loudly and long that the conversation to follow would drown in my raging inner fire-dragon, but of course, to the outside, I put on a smile to cover my blood boiling truth and decided to play it cool.

It turned out that the girl wasn't talented at all, and I had known it right from the start. After failing and failing to get the right emotions out of her, Stefan finally had the "brilliant" idea to swap the parts. That was the end of the girls' participation and the play. Stefan and I kept in touch, and from then on, we also "pretended to be friends."

A few weeks later, he suddenly started to confide in me about a girl he adored. And this time, he confessed, he was also, for a change, interested in a committed relationship, not an open one. It hurt me so much, but instead of walking away, I found myself in the same situation I had been in with David.

The girl he was smitten with was stick-thin. That was the only apparent reason I could find as to why he would not want to commit to me. I needed to take the diet a notch more seriously. I needed to show him that I could be stick-thin, too. I needed him to regret his wrong choices.

Why did I have the urge to want him back? Why, why, why? Status, ego-boost, and not wanting to be alone, the wrong reasons - the human intuition is finely tuned. If we do things that hurt us, and we just ignore it, it can lead us to forget how to use it. My intuition regarding Stefan, from the first moment on had been a clear and loud "Alarm!"

CLUSTER-FUCK

~ The Picture of Dorian Gray ~

The most ironic turn of events in Stefan's and my time spent together was that one day when he bought me a book about borderline-syndrome and Narcissism. He smiled and was excited: this would surely help ME.

The title already made me swallow hard, and as soon as I browsed through the pages, I got shaky knees. Was this finally someone having the guts to tell me the truth about me? Was it that that had been wrong with me the whole time?

I took this very seriously and decided to withdraw from activities and social engagements. A soul-searching trip began, but unfortunately, not further towards the light, but darkness.

As a result, all the self-confidence I had left, vanished in its entirety. Without doubt or resistance, I bought into Stefan's diagnosis and began to accept that I was a nut job. My disturbed eating behavior and lying to everyone about why I was losing weight and where all the food went, were proving it.

The combination of bingeing and purging wasn't the odd emergency remedy anymore but had started to become a regular habit. I had begun to use food like a drug instead of enjoying it, and I carefully planned out sessions when I needed relief. There was clearly something very wrong with me. Who does something like this - this disgusting type of thing?

When I started to read the book, it made sense why Stefan would think this way about me. It talked about people who would believe that they were talented, and who had feelings of genius and greatness about themselves. It also talked about anger issues, those people had. Yes, I got more and more worried when I read that.

With the intention to "manage my narcissism," I decided that I would need to radically step in the background. That suited me quite well because despite the thrill I got from outstanding achievements, I wasn't a fan of praise at all. It embarrassed me when I won a painting or writing competition, or if a teacher pointed out how excellent my homework was and all eyes were on red faced me. Public praise always made me blush, and that showed weakness, and I wanted it to pass fast.

The book stated that narcissists were unwilling to recognize or identify, i.e., empathize with the feelings and needs of others and that they believe that others are envious of him or her.

Because I had allowed Stefan to make me believe these statements, I never again utilized my talents as joyously as I had before. Instead, I started to feel not only embarrassed by achievements and praise, but also almost ashamed of it.

I hated my whole self now, including my creativity, the last thing I had always been able to cling to.

Only years later would I understand what had happened to me. Since I have always journaled, I have the proof, in black and white, that the things, my boyfriends used to tell me were WRONG WITH ME, were WRONG WITH THEM. Behaviors that the most toxic people accused me of were often the very specific traits that they exhibited themselves. Unfortunately, I did not really fully understand what "projection" means and how it works. Forgiveness, however, is the perfect looking-glass. I wonder if Stefan ever considered being a narcissist himself.

I firmly believe that we indeed CAN read each other and that we can figure out each other's truth instantly. If we only wanted to. Because most of the time, we choose to look at the mask. But if you look behind the façade and see with your heart, you can read sadness, fear, and sickness in people all the time. We just have to open our eyes. And then, it is the more significant effort to empathize with the pain of others without getting dragged into their drama.

Stefan was not far off in terms of the intensity of what was brewing behind MY mask. Narcissism, eating disorders, and depression are in similar ball-parks. With this new secret thing that I started doing to look thin, I had proved to myself that I was indeed mentally ill: a two-faced liar who was only concerned about her looks. On top of all this, I also now felt disgusted by myself. This disgusting thing I was doing needed to end immediately and for good. However, for some reason, not like with Vera where I could just turn around and confess, this time, I couldn't stop. It was too tempting to have a "session" when the world seemed too stressful. It felt freeing to binge on everything and anything without worrying about calories or putting on weight. Calorie-counting, by the way, had become one of my hopeless attempts to get a handle on my eating behavior. I memorized a whole calorie booklet. But even if I would stick to low-calorie food, I would not lose weight, and couldn't resist the urge to binge and purge.

For me, this gross and mad thing I was doing was my safety net, my only control in the sense that I could do whatever I wanted without fearing the results. But my mind went back and forth on it. Before a binge, I would tell myself that I had nothing to worry about since this was the thing that supposedly everyone who was smart did. After a binge and purge, I was not so sure about that anymore.

I also allowed Stefan to continue the squeezing and squashing of my already wounded heart. One night, he kissed me, and I began to fantasize a little bit about us getting back together. While we had a drink in a bar, he told me in a throwaway side sentence, that he had been sleeping with that Munster gallery Renate "now and then." He confessed that he also had sex with her during our "relationship" - he even slept with her during the visit to Munster I wrote about earlier.

I felt like someone had just taken my guts out and hit me with a sledgehammer on the head. Stefan continued about how much he was missing her, now that he didn't live in Munster anymore, adding that he was glad that "at least" I was here, his "rainbow!?".

As usual, instead of screaming at him, I reacted as if I couldn't care less. But it hurt so badly inside. I just swallowed it all up, allowing it to rage in me. As soon as I got home, I took it out on a giant binge where I devoured a whole cake and a pint of ice-cream. The purge was violent. As my stomach emptied itself into the toilet bowl, I felt like I was staring into the pain that I wasn't able to handle. I cried bitterly as soon as I was done.

I would find myself trapped with my new dark and secretive habit, intensifying itself with each time I did it, until the end of the year approached. Strangely, it made all my other problems move into the background and less relevant.

Stefan and I spent one more New Year's evening together. Later on, during that night, we lost each other at a party, and when I tried to find him, someone told me that he had seen Stefan kissing someone. Of course, that "someone" had to be a person I knew, too. I reacted as if it didn't matter, and decided to find someone else to kiss, also. This was the end of the chapter Stefan, and I never spoke to him again.

In the three months following the end of this relationship, my binge and purge sessions exploded from planned out sessions on the side to purging the first family meals, too. Who cared about Stefan. Within another week, I would now do it after every meal with my folks. I thought that I might as well fully commit to this new thing since I couldn't stop it anyways. More and more people began to ask me if I had lost some weight. It felt great.

More positive experiences came along with my new self-confidence: Someone who had seen my portrait work at school asked me if I wanted to have an exhibit of my art in a gallery they owned. Sadly, because I firmly believed that I was a narcissist, I didn't feel happy but pressured instead. I voiced doubts about being the right person to ask for an exhibit. I confessed that I didn't have any great oil paintings or anything, but the friendly inquirer eased my worries. He assured me that he thought my sketches and style were great, and he would trust in anything I would create.

I ended up agreeing to do it. My parents were proud and offered our cellar as a work-space to me. They also sponsored the colors and the canvasses.

The first painting I created was a portrait of Stefan in yellow and blue. I integrated a poem with a line in it saying, "seeing, smelling, touching, I dive into you, searching for the grounds." I named it "Dorian," after the famous Oscar Wilde novel that I found quite fitting.

It looked appealing, but I hated it and painted over it with black. The experience of trying to find my theme turned out to be a hair-pulling exercise. I spent hours and hours in this 300-year-old medieval catacomb with its 12-foot ceiling.

At one point, after I had painted yet again over another half-finished painting with black, just like I did before with Stefan's portrait, I had the fantastic idea to take a tape recorder downstairs, and I put on some Tracy Chapman. This tape should turn out to be the only soundtrack I would listen to over, and over again. And suddenly it was there – the concept!

It started with sky sceneries to ease my mind, and suddenly I thought, "Sweet Sixteen. That's going to be the title. I am going to create a visual diary."

Fancy clouds in the most beautiful yellows, purples, orange, blues, but also greens, black, and reds shaped the expression of my different moods and feelings that I wasn't letting out. At a later point, I layered shadows on top. How symbolic, layering shadows of myself over the beautiful colorful skies. My grey thoughts and the unsolvable puzzle of being earth-bound, i.e., having to die and leave all beautiful moments behind one day anyway, had surfaced in my art.

Amid the painting period, I also landed a gig as a singer in a band. A guitarist spoke to me at the "Knockout." He had once heard me sing at a jam session with friends. He told me that I had impressed him and that he wanted to start a band project. His idea was a kind of Rap/Funk thing which I loved. He asked me if I could write lyrics, and I was thrilled about the opportunity to write. There were three older professional players (guitar, drums, and bass), and four younger musicians, two vocals (myself and another guy), a DJ, and a keyboardist. The concept was brilliant, and we put the stakes high. Our goal was to have the first concert with original songs in precisely four months.

How much more stress could I have put on my shoulders? To be able to deal with my workload, the purge and binge-loads reached a new peak. Now I would even go on extra shopping trips. I was almost proud of my devious ways, going on those shopping trips with the money I had stolen from my mum. No one had a clue. I could do whatever I wanted.

While I had lost a little weight in the beginning, my face got puffy, and I felt bloated all the time. My weight had also plateaued somewhere, definitely not even close to dream-body. As we all know, the initial weight-loss is a lie. It's just water, i.e., dehydration.

I was amazed at how much my body could accomplish without getting tired. The more I ran on empty, the more energy I seemed to have. That intrigued me, and I wondered if I was running on some sort of emergency setting. I didn't feel stressed or tired. Was I not able to decipher my emotions anymore? My massive levels of anxiety simply washed up unseen on the shores of my private, remote island: my eating disorder.

Another piece of emotional driftwood was that my old piano teacher died. To distract myself from this loss, I had started to try myself out with Jazz instead of the classical piano. This helped me with composing some songs for the band, too.

My father, who used to be a saxophonist himself, believed in my musical talent and had used his contacts to find a stellar teacher, this famous and fantastic Jazz pianist. I told my dad that I thought I was not good enough for that teacher, but I didn't want to disappoint him either.

My parents are truly loving, kind, and supportive people, and to see them happy was incredibly important to me. I auditioned for the teacher, and to my surprise, he accepted me as his student. I, however, still thought that I wasn't good enough because even if I was able to play the songs, I didn't know what I was doing because I had taught myself by ear. I didn't understand the music theory with harmonies on the paper. He gave me a lot of theoretical homework, and I wasn't even able to verbalize my concerns. I didn't have the musical vocabulary needed.

At home, I proved to myself how utterly incapable of writing harmonies on a piece of paper I was. There it was. Proof. I did not understand a darn thing. It made me feel helpless, and dumb, to sit there and not understand a word. Ah well. Nothing new. I threw my hands in the air, claiming to be a lazy loser and stopped trying to figure it out. The TV and bingeing on food helped to quiet the nagging guilt.

Needless to say, that the piano teacher experience failed. I quit and stayed away from playing the piano altogether for a long time with the odd exception. It is sad to observe, what a lousy self-image I had, and how I put myself down, how nothing that I did was ever good enough in my own eyes.

Thinking poorly about ourselves is one of the main reasons for giving up. It deprives us of our passion, excitement, fun, curiosity, and makes it impossible to envision success, which is a formula for failure.

Besides my prematurely aborted attempt to get serious about playing the piano, I still had enough other activities to keep me distracted from having to deal with myself. My exhibition had been a success, and I had sales, great newspaper coverage, and got hired to create some custom pieces.

I was relieved that my' image in town' seemed to be on the upswing, as my eating disorder spiralled further DOWN. The stress to juggle the band, the artwork, theatre, and trying to keep up with school had triggered off a real rampage. Now, my eating disorder seemed to GIVE me energy, not just mentally, but physically.

I now needed to do IT many times a day to feel normal. I was hooked on the feeling of starvation, i.e., ketosis, to get me into overdrive. Being hyped up by caffeine helped me to power through my schedule.

The foods I binged on had become very sugary and more in volume. My insulin levels must have gone through the roof. I binged until I got light-headed and sick. There was no half-way of doing this anymore. I ran from one project to the next, always a quick stop at the toilet bowl in between. I could encounter as many problems as I wanted.

The purging was something that I believed to have control over, and it felt safe to break all the rules (eating as much unhealthy foods as I wanted), and not having to pay for it (gaining weight - becoming a "target"). It felt like performing a naughty magic trick that purging could reverse back. I could taste all the forbidden flavors of all the gummi-bears, ice-cream, cookies, cake, bread, cheeses, whatever I wanted. I could stuff myself full to the brim and still be in control. But then, after a while, I began to wonder if I was really calling the shots. Would life without it even still be possible?

Trying to envision life without my secret habit made me tremble, and I forced myself to think this thought to the end: the answer was NO. Wow. I realized that I somehow just raced passed the exit without even noticing it a long time ago.

I tried to envision what my stomach must look like from the inside. I knew that I was stretching it more and more and that my binge attacks became bigger and bigger, as well. I also realized, that there was a correlation between stress-levels and doing it. Had I turned into an early workaholic?

I needed validation so badly at the time, yet I was unable to accept any of it. I felt as if I had to make up for all my failures, hoping that people, especially my parents, would finally understand me. It made me feel utterly sad to see my parents being helpless when it came to parenting, and disciplining me. My former heroes were saddened by me and unbeknownst to them, entirely out of options in regards to influencing me.

My beautiful parents meant it all so very well, yet, I do not recall a serious attempt to listen to what I needed. Of all the factors I could think of, the one that hurt me most was that they lost their trust in me. At the time, it almost felt as if they had forgotten who I was. They were horrified, scared, and disturbed by me.

IF YOU ARE A LOVED ONE, OR A FRIEND OF SOMEONE WHO STRUGGLES WITH ADDICTION, NEVER STOP ASKING HOW YOUR LOVED ONE FEELS OR IF HE/SHE NEEDS ANYTHING, no matter how old, or difficult they are. Show them you care, but do not judge or tell them what to do. Just be there. Hold space. Checking in like this without applying pressure can fail a thousand times, but there might be that one moment where a person with a dark secret will eventually take a leap of faith.

From today's perspective, as a mother of two kids, I will keep in mind that no matter how tough it might get, I want my kids to know that I love them, no matter what. I will try my best to make space to listen to them and their needs. Even when puberty strikes! Open and honest communication is the binding glue for families and friendships.

Back then, I wasn't sure about being loved anymore. All I saw was the disappointment and the grim faces at home. At the same time, I tried to cope with my first breakup, my first exhibition, my first professional music project, my first failure at school, and becoming the vice-president of our school's student body. Yes, that happened at the same time, and to my surprise as well. Students didn't seem to mind other students who just had to repeat a year and be losers? This fact didn't make sense to me, but I took on the prestigious role – and all that additional workload, too.

After school, as soon as I entered home, I dropped my bags, had lunch, threw it up, and then painted, prepared for a student event, or wrote a song. Then, I would usually smoke a couple of cigarettes out of my window and wait until my mother had to go to school to teach the afternoon classes. As soon as the door fell into the lock, I turned on the TV for an hour, got my baguette and the hazelnut spread, ate it all in 5-10 minutes, and purged. Once the toilet was flushed and I had brushed my teeth, I went back to work. About an hour later, I had another binge-purge session with whatever was available and wouldn't be missed by anyone.

With this regularity, I eased into my eating disorder – the horror about what I was doing had worn off. This is the time where I probably began to study myself more consciously.

This is a critical piece of information for you, too, if you are struggling with an eating disorder. If you are already used to your eating disorder, and you are not in "freefall mode" anymore, where you surprise yourself daily with how much worse it can get, you have already mastered a vital step. It is some sort of stabilization of your situation and also a de-dramatization.

These moments where the self-hate and horror levels are down, are the gaps you can use to put your neutral lab coat on and to take out your notebook.

What's your pattern?

During the time where I had found my groove with the ED, this is what I did. I started with moments of being amazed at what Humans are willing to do to cope.

Going general, as in seeing myself as a human in my ED life, rather than just the individual, "Anabelle," yielded some sort of neutral clarity.

How mind-boggling it was that someone could pull off this type of secret while life seemed to be back on track from the outside. The choice to become an actress indeed inspired and aided this helpful switch of my perspective.

With my "observer-goggles" on, I noticed that I had a pattern of needing to reward myself. It seemed to be co-related with my trauma of having been misunderstood, as in having to repeat a class despite being highly gifted, for example. I also realized that watching the most brainless content on TV probably felt so good to me because I was so deep in the intellectual realms with my books and plays. Mainstream TV content programming gave me a break from thinking and also a connection to the "real world" out there.

Was this healthy? No. But it was helping me somehow. It was a crutch. It became clear to me that stuffing my face with food and purging it afterward was a trap - a prison. It all had started with a diet, but now I needed this behavior to stop. I wanted to be healthy. I interpreted my compulsive behavior as the need to unleash all my anger.

What does one do if one is locked up in a place and can't get out? The only thing I thought I could do at the time as a practical and immediate step one was to get a handle on the psychological side because my body did this now without me having a say anymore.

A song came to my mind, "Die Gedanken Sind Frei," a song we talked about in school that concentration camp prisoners had been singing… it's meaning was that thoughts are free-flowing. That one can choose them. Since there was no point in continuing to do this while beating myself up, I decided that I would at least try my best not to engage in all the inner self-hate and loser dialogue I had with myself after purging. There was simply no point since I was doing it anyways.

The more I did it, the more my body got confused and started to suck out every nutritional ingredient from the foods I binged on that it could store. Especially fat, I suppose, which is so significant for a healthy body and which is the Anti-Christ for people struggling with eating disorders. I felt that my body was sucking up fat during my binges like a vacuum cleaner. It seemed like it got used to this kind of war-time and developed a system to obtain and store quicker than usual what it wanted.

The initial experience of losing weight had stopped a while ago, and I realized that the trap described above, was this never-ending diet to keep the pounds down, in addition to bingeing and purging.

Even with a changed perspective, it was hard. I tried out not to binge as often, but I couldn't stop my urges to purge. Everything landed in the toilet bowl, even healthy foods. When I tried to stop purging, I felt so fat and heavy. My body was not used to keeping it in anymore. It was horrible on one hand, but on the other hand, I would like to observe this from a different angle via asking you a question, my dear reader: isn't it also brilliant, this little machine that we inherit by birth?

Years later, well advanced in trying to decode my eating disorder, I asked myself: If the body adapts to bad habits and creates a system to get what it wants, it inevitably also adopts the good ones!

Don't you think your body naturally strongly prefers to be healthy again? I mean entirely healthy, which includes the joy of eating? It does.

Let's face it: it takes some nerve to bring yourself to this dark and vile act. Eating like a pig, and showering yourself with your bail afterward, keeping the lie up, and trying to be perfect all the time is not easy.

I'm not sarcastic, I mean it. People who get drawn to this, at least the ones I know, including myself, are hungry in more than physical ways. They thirst for life and its secrets; they WANT to, and they HAVE to try things out. They want to get to the bottom of the matter. They are usually people who blame themselves first. That means that they have a social attitude and reflect a lot.

As we are all mirrors for each other, let's continue with precisely that, the reflections.

CHEATERS!

As time passed, my love-life resurfaced from the land of the dead in the shape of Peter, a handsome young chap from a different school.

From today's perspective, it is almost amusing to see how I picked myself a trophy boyfriend with Peter. He was handsome to look at, but inside, he was a mess. Just like me, he was through and through depressed. While I had my ED and drinking, he used to soothe his pain with smoking dope all day. I remember deliberately CHOOSING him - I didn't fall in love. I CHOSE him because he was "Mr. Popular" at his school. There he was now, sitting in my room, looking desperate for a hug, a kiss, a relationship. I remember thinking, "alright, why not. At least everyone will be jealous."

This emotionally disconnected mindset would last for three and ½ years. Peter was not all bad. He was definitely smart and sensitive, but OH MY GOD, nobody approved of him, including myself. He was one of those overly honest people that give a sh** about other people's feelings. I knew this state of being well since I had been through his phase after coming clean with Vera. But in Peter's case, the "honesty," and "straight-forwardness" was full-on rude, if not cruel. Full stop.

Whether Peter was aware of it or not, he insulted my friends, my parents, and of course, myself regularly. I didn't like this aspect of him, but since this was my first exclusive relationship, I cut him some slack. And beyond that, I thought I could save him because I understood his pain and radical-honesty-thing. Also, best of all, focusing on him made me forget about my own problems.

We had a very physical relationship, but it seemed tricky to extend our exclusivity to the realm of fleshy endeavors as well: about three months in, Peter confessed that he had cheated on me with his ex-girlfriend.

Something went off again in my head, but not in a healthy way - let's call it Stefan-trauma. I immediately went back to what I knew: cheating as a revenge act. Not only once. Whenever it happened, I would arrange a meeting with Peter the next day and explain the situation.

I thought that my honesty was my free ticket. I would casually tell him that I was sorry, that I would understand if he wanted to break up with me, but he always forgave me. This spiel would continue until I betrayed him with his best friend. Yikes.

Peter and his best friend William used to smoke a lot of weed together, about five times the amount that Peter and I would. They drowned their worries about their future with it as well. Both had just started grade 12 and were classmates, and in the process of trying to figure out what they wanted to do after school but were clueless.

Because of these existential decisions that needed to be made, Peter steered towards a proper little crisis where he would stay in bed for days and cry. He was so down that he bought himself a ticket to India, hoping for a spiritual miracle. I fully supported Peter with his India trip, but he went there at a difficult time in my life.

At this point, I had a particularly bad relationship with my parents and teachers. It was almost as bad as the year before, where I had to repeat a year. This time it would come close to me wanting to drop out of school entirely because, as a part of my self-examination, I realized that I wanted to go to a drama school, instead of going to university.

Unlike Peter and William, I knew what I wanted to do. I had experienced my calling years prior. I was sure that this was my path and my inner voice was so strong, saying "NOW, NOW, NOW, DO IT NOW, NOW - you are so full of energy and passion for it, later on, it will just be more difficult, you will be older and have the weight of your A-levels on your shoulders! Staying another three years at school will take the wind out of your sails…"

My inner voice was right, but my surroundings seemed to clash against it. I was conditioned to please and felt I needed to do what other people wanted from me at that time in my life. I think that was also the main reason for my rebellion in the shape of my secret and late-night drinking tours: it was to get rid of other people's expectations of me and to buy me freedom by doing it. It was some kind of shock-therapy for all of us. For me, my friends, my family, my teachers, my enemies, and the rest of my world.

So, Peter was off to India, and he had asked me to drop off some weed at William's place. He didn't want it to go bad while he was away for the two months that he would spend riding on elephants and seeking salvation in ashrams, temples, and bathing in the Ganges. We called the place where William lived "W-Street."

W-Street was some sort of live-action Sesame-street for the dazed and confused. William's crazy, huge, 4-bedroom apartment was a big chaotic mess, meeting point and party haven for all sorts of people like me and best of all: it was open 24/7.

Once I had set foot in William's pad for the first time, I would spend every free minute there. I was always welcome. There was way too much to laugh about NOT to spend every free minute there - and it also included free pot to smoke.

After yet another party night with lots of movie watching and even more piff-paff, I started to have a first sleepover. As I was trying to escape the pressure at home, staying there almost made me feel like a whole person again.

The BEST thing about staying at William's place was that there was no possibility to purge. I just couldn't do it there. I couldn't fathom that William could catch me, and weirdly enough, I didn't even feel the urge to binge there either. But although there were first improvements related to my eating disorder, the problems at school and with my parents pushed me further towards a breaking point.

I started to avoid going to school again, but this time I didn't care anymore about fabricating excuses or trying to avoid consequences. If they kicked me out, all my problems would be solved, and I could go to drama school. But I was not one hundred percent behind this step because of the anguish I would need to put my parents through. They so desperately wanted me to get my A-Levels (those important finals that make you eligible to go to university).

I knew that I needed to make a choice - and I needed to make it soon before I would get suspended from school. Ideally, I wanted to leave, not be kicked out. Déjavu: Just like the first time around, my parents were in a new panic again. This time, however, they were fully informed about my non-compliance at school right away. But unfortunately, they didn't even know where I was sleeping anymore. I had disappeared. I only went home when I knew that my parents weren't there. I changed my clothes, told my grandmother that I was okay. Good girl.

My father, who freaked out about my disappearance, studied all my notes at home and found some pot, as well as David's address. He went there, David opened, my father explained the situation and David said: "You know what? That's not okay that Anabelle is putting you through this. Let's find her. I know a lot of people in town…"

David and my dad went to a few coffee shops and had the information about my whereabouts within 20 minutes. That's the "small town syndrome." Everybody knows everything about everyone. The secret service of small-towners works better than Scotland Yard and the FBI together. If my father had known that David had introduced me to pot, drinking, and rebellion in the first place, he probably would have never contacted him.

The phone rang at W-Street. William answered and walked to the lounge and said, "your father." I was astounded that he had found out William's number. Almost flattered that he had gone to all this effort to find me. I answered and confessed that I had concluded that I wanted to leave school and that my dad should not worry.

Well, I think these two concepts didn't fit into a logical sentence for his understanding. After a moment of silence, it made "click." He hung up. Urgh. I couldn't pull through with it. I knew it at that very moment.

The next morning, I called my school. I had the secretary on the line. She knew me. I was the infamous girl that only caused trouble. I asked her to connect me with the headmaster. When he answered, I told him that I wanted to have something like a private meeting with him, and he scheduled an appointment in the afternoon.

A few hours later, I found myself sitting down with a cup of coffee in his office and explained the following: "I'm sorry. I'm in a kind of existential crisis, you see. I know I want to be an actress and nothing else, but I'm still at school. My parents are both teachers, and I know that A-Levels are important - more to them than me, I guess - but that is still causing me trouble to make decisions. Do you think that having my A-Level and going to university will help me in the end with an acting career? Now I have the energy to go to all these auditions - I'm on fire, do you understand, Mr. Kolico? What are the consequences if I drop out of school now? What would you recommend?"

Mr. Kolico took a deep breath, and to my surprise, there wasn't a single bad word coming out of his mouth. He told me that I only had another 2 ½ years ahead of me, which wasn't that much. If I wanted to do my A-Levels at a later point, it would be about the same, maybe three years, but if I wanted to study, my freedom of choice would be a little limited, he told me. He said: "Listen, if you want to continue, we can work something out with the hours you missed so far. If you, however, HAVE to leave, I wish you the best of luck, too. You're a smart girl, and the teachers think highly of you."

What?? The teachers thought highly of me? I had been so full of trauma and aggravation towards the school that my anger alone would have propelled me out like a helicopter into the new future. But now? Some teachers thought highly of me?!

I went "home-home," because I felt the desperate need to have a bath. I needed to think. When I arrived, my mom was sitting on the table, crying. As I entered, she looked up for a second with these troubled eyes, then she got up without saying a word and left the room. Her eyes confirmed it, just like a good look into a squeaky clean mirror, that I wasn't ready to put another dagger in my parents' chests. I just couldn't leave this place in chaos like that. I had to clean this mess up.

I heard my parents talk and leave the house. I had three big binge-purge sessions in a row as soon as the door had fallen into the lock. Then I took out my school books and glimpsed over what I had missed during the last few weeks.

The next day I went to school, apologized to every teacher, and continued as if nothing ever happened. And going to school would continue for me for the next 2 ½ years. I would just grin and bear it, and kept on emptying my parents' fridge and pantry to help me with the bear-it part.

All of these events took place, while Peter was still in India. He didn't have a clue what was going on with me, searching for Samadhi. I promised my parents not to have a sleepover at William's place at W-Street anymore, but I'd still visit William now and then. William and I both only realized how much we needed each other when we weren't around each other that often anymore.

When I stopped sleeping over, I noticed that William started to drink much more than he used to. William drank so excessively during the next few weeks, that he would wake up the next afternoon, with a blackout, amidst some furniture that he had destroyed. I knew that he had fallen in love with me, and I realized that I had fallen in love with him, but because there was my boyfriend Peter, trying to cure his depression in India, there was no future for us. I regretted that I had crossed a barrier by being around him all that time.

A weekend later, I bumped into him at the Knockout. He bought me a drink, and we talked, joked, philosophized, and had a great time. Even though both of us knew what would happen, he asked me to have a drink with him at his place.

I told myself that all was innocent, as always and that if anything, I would maybe just spend one last night there to say goodbye to all the happy times spent at W-Street. When we arrived, he asked me if I could hold him, and I wanted nothing else but that. And then we made love. Deep down, we felt intense relief to have finally slept with each other. It reminded me of the feelings I had after throwing up, but just like in the eating department, a massive pang of colossal guilt followed afterward. I had never lied to Peter about an affair, but I knew that I had to keep this one as a secret. It was such a horrible thing to do to Peter. He looked up to William.

I told Peter on the phone that I had spent quite a few nights at Williams's place, and he trusted me completely. William didn't take the results of our last night together lightly, either. Just like me, he was riddled with feelings of guilt and reached some sort of a downward "peak". As a result, he drank even more than the weeks before, if that was possible at all. I didn't know what to do with my lousy conscience either and cut the contact for a while. Peter came back, sitting on cloud nine, spiritually recharged and motivated, while I felt like a swine. But no worries, I should get the karmic response soon after.

My bulimia had taken on a different shape, yet again. I had accepted that I was trapped and binged and purged with a lot less self-hatred, which was definitely an improvement. Since I had decided to finish school, I tried my hardest to control my urges as much as I could. My new desperate attempt to get a handle on the bingeing and purging was to experiment with "only throwing up in batches."

I realized that there were more patterns, for example, that I always binged and purged more often when I was on my own at home. Another epiphany came to me: when I cooked something for myself, I didn't purge either. Sometimes, if I managed to cook my lunch and not hang out in front of the TV while no one was at home, I was even able not to do it for a few days! But every time I thought I had found the "trick," the bulimia would always come back. And a large piece of the puzzle that I couldn't get a handle on was that when I didn't purge, I packed on the pounds rapidly.

As a result, I would start a new diet and sports regime, but disappointed myself and slipped back into my easy go-to thing to do. Peter also added some fuel to my desire to binge and purge. I remember, for example, when he and I sat in a café. I felt beautiful that day, something I didn't feel often.

I was wearing a body-hugging white dress and had my hair pinned up in an elegant up-do. We had lunch on the sunny terrace. All seemed good when suddenly a skinny girl, eating a carrot, passed by. Peter said: Can't you be a bit more like her? Look? She is beautiful and thin. She is eating carrots.

I believe I weighed around 63 kg/135 pounds at this time, and I am 5'9 tall, oh well. I mentioned before, that Peter had that "gift" of being overly-honest-rude. That indeed hadn't changed after India. Peter was, by the way, the first person that I vaguely told that I had a bad relationship with my body. Maybe he intended to inspire me - perhaps he only wanted me to feel happy in my skin and made a stupid comment only guys can make. It doesn't matter, it's over, and in the past, that's a fact.

Fact for me back then was that I had yet more proof that I was a fat cow and not right. The carrot-girl comment hurt me a lot. As a result, I promised myself to give up trying to fight my bulimia until I had either figured out how not to gain weight or until I was that far down the spiral that I would be able to allow myself to get fat happily. Now was not the time, so I regressed to the few-times-a-day-schedule.

Tapping into the past, I can still feel my bad self-image of the old days. The daily fights that you might know yourself - the diets, the failures, the looks in every mirror to check if it is true or not, that I was fat. You probably know what it looks like and feels like to slip again and again and again. Bulimia is so much more about a broken heart than about calorie lists, and the daily battle to purge without getting caught.

Peter finished his A-Levels and moved to Berlin, the place where I wanted to live as well after I finished school. But what could I do: I had another two years ahead of me until I could leave this town, so we started a long-distance relationship. In a way, this distance between us helped me to focus on school, and regular phone calls, as well as letters, kept us going. But I felt a declining effort on his side. "He must feel swamped, trying to get settled at Uni," is what I thought.

One night, a few weeks after he moved to Berlin, I met a friend in a bar. She lived in the same area as Peter's parents, and she told me that she had seen him outside his house this afternoon. Excuse me, what? I mean, I was his girlfriend, and he didn't tell me when he was coming home for a visit?! I asked her if she was sure and she answered that she was - unfortunately.

I ordered another drink and tried to call him, but no one answered - it was already late at night. My friend gave me a ride to the northern part of the little town, and I climbed over the fence. I threw stones on his window, nothing. I was intoxicated and angry, so I decided (oy!!!!) to climb up a wooden railing that was equipped to support roses - not Humans.

Well, in my case, it let one big and drunk rose fall quite hard on her bottom. I caused a spectacle, involving not only Peter's parents but also Peter's neighbors, who were standing on their balconies, asking if they should phone the police... they asked ME - how polite.

I said that I was okay and went to the front entrance and rang the doorbell. Peter's father opened. He was NOT pleased to see a disheveled me at this late hour after I caused this racket outside. Sleepovers weren't appreciated, either. Peter came downstairs and took me up to his room, scolding me for how crazy and impossible I was. Well… yes, I must admit that he was right this time. I fell asleep like a stone as he was still yelling at me.

As a prompt result of this night, we split up during a fiery word-match in the morning. I didn't understand anything anymore. This disaster had come out of the blue.

Peter went back to Berlin, and I changed my mind about splitting up. I needed to talk sense into him! I called, he answered, and to my surprise, he seemed apologetic for not telling me about his last visit home. He also regretted splitting up and tried to justify his brash decision with the embarrassment that I had caused him in front of his parents and the whole neighborhood - a fair point. He admitted that lately, the stress of making ends meet with his new apartment in Berlin had gotten to him. In a side sentence, he mentioned that he had decided to rent out a room to a girl from our hometown, who also wanted to be an actress and had just moved to Berlin. I knew her and I didn't like her. As usual, while I was boiling inside, I kept my cool and wished Peter the best of luck with this decision and pretended that this wasn't a big deal. We ended the call with the amicable agreement to give ourselves time to think about how we wanted to proceed from here. Two weeks of silence followed.

The next time Peter came down to visit his parents, he gave me a call, and we met for a beer. He had missed me. I asked outright if Peter had an affair with the girl that had moved in. According to him, I was paranoid and jealous, and then he kissed me and asked for forgiveness for breaking up with me the last time – and whoops, we were back together. Yep.

He went back to Berlin, and I hopped on a train to visit him a week later. On my way to the city of my dreams, I experienced a spiritual moment. As I wrote into my journal, wondering, as usual, what life was all about, I heard a voice coming from a few seats further back. It was so deep, smooth, charismatic, and spoke such a beautiful German that I had to get up and see to which person this magical voice belonged.

138

Right at the moment, when I spotted a glimpse of the voice's owner, he said to another person: "There are things between heaven and earth that we can't see. We can only feel them. But just because we can't see or understand them, it doesn't mean they don't exist. Everything is vibration and waves. And these waves could be anything. Where do they go? Why do they exist? Where do they come from?"

The man was talking about God. At that moment, I knew that his message was for me. It hit the spot, and even if it doesn't make sense for you, beloved reader, for me, at that moment, it did.

Inspired, I wrote down his quote in my diary, wondering if I was still an atheist. Were atheists even more stupid than believers? Had I wasted valuable time to find out what was shaping the world around us by throwing any thought of God's existence in the trash? Had I allowed a medium-bright classmate to become my "God," by believing that faith was only for primitive people suffering from a thunder-God-confusion-idiocy? Indeed, thunder DID come from electric fields, yes, but where did the electric fields come from? Right, very likely not from a man with a white beard that created the world in seven days, but science keeps on looking and only finds more questions. If the big bang caused the creation of the universe, then what had caused did the big-bang?

I decided on that day to become an agnostic and that I wanted to stick with the teachings of Socrates. The only thing I knew was that I didn't know anything. Including my ideas about death. Could I be sure that death was this big black, meaningless nothing?

One thing was for sure: When I had accepted that terrible, empty, black nothingness as our final destination, every particle of my life had turned into black oblivion, too. I realized that I had lived without any purpose - driven only by worldly, instant gratification. And inspired by this realization, that I didn't know anything, paired with my willingness to open my mind, I decided that I wanted to find out how to open the most crucial door again: my heart.

I took a new leap of faith in something. The truth, purpose, meaning, the innate knowing of goodness and kindness, the source of all cosmic intelligence, the well, the source, the creator, God, call it what you like.

From that moment on, a new search began. In the beginning, it was a passive one, starting with my acceptance and tolerance of other people's beliefs without the need to judge or devalue them. Later, it turned into a search within. I figured that all I had to do was to listen to the strings of my heart. If their pull produced beautiful music, i.e., positive feelings, all I needed to do was stop, listen, and try to get more of it. But it is still a little piece from where we are in the story and hearing divine melodies of my heart.

Seeing Peter in Berlin was so different this time. He was surprisingly lovely and sensitive, and for once NOT only concerned about himself and his depression. It astounded me most that he didn't even smoke a single joint. That night, he took me out to a fancy restaurant to celebrate my arrival in town. I ordered an ostrich steak, and we chatted away like two lovebirds. Suddenly, like lightning in my head and between a bite of steak and laughter, I asked him: "Did you fuck your roommate?"

I don't know where that came from. I hadn't thought about it. I hadn't planned to ask this question and especially not in such a harsh way, either. It just popped up in my mind like a flash, like a sudden brain fart. I just threw it out there without any context, in the middle of an absolutely unrelated and otherwise great conversation.

Peter just looked at me and blushed. When the time for an honest "no" had already passed, I knew that the only answer embedded in his silence was a YES. I asked: "Once? A couple of times?" - "A couple of times," was his answer.

I put my knife and fork down, smiled at the waiter, and ordered the bill, asked for change, went to the cigarette machine, and got two packs. Without looking, I went outside and walked, walked, walked, for an hour. It was in the middle of winter. He followed me, but we didn't speak a word. I finally arrived at his place, and waited silently, gave him a sign to open the door, went up and put on my nightgown.

As it started to snow, I stepped out on the balcony and sat there for another half an hour. I couldn't feel the cold. He was looking at me through the window and urged me to come inside until I finally listened. Still not saying a word, I took out my sketchbook and wrote down with a black marker all that was going through my mind. It was a tirade of me wanting to chop off their heads and more rolled out on the paper in angry, large, black letters.

For the first time, I had expressed my true feelings somehow, instead of swallowing them. All this vile, dark, terrible stuff came out on paper. I felt better, closed the book, looked at him, and said: "Tell her that I know." And that was all that there was to talk about for that night.

Was this the revenge of the universe for all that I had done wrong? I forgave him. The relationship was dead, though, even if we thought we had come a long way, also if we were very tolerant and forgiving this time. My opinion until today is that if you have messed around, there's hardly a way back when you have an extensive cheating record. Being a cheat is like being a thief or a bully. Sure, we can always find reasons why we do certain things, but there is a clear voice in us that tells us it isn't right. What a price I paid for those simple lessons.

MADNESS

~ Dad's Lunch on the Wall ~

Back home, still in my long-distance relationship to Peter, creeping on its last legs, and my eating disorder going on, as usual, I met Eddy.

Eddy. Finally, here is the first man who brought love and laughter to my life, my real first love. He was my guy, a dream come true, the one where you stare at each other and can't believe that life has brought you together because for you, he is the kindest and most adorable person, and you are the same in his eyes.

Eddy had seen me for the first time at one of our band's concerts. He worked in my favorite bar in town, and I saw him put up a sticker of my music group. I commented on it, and he quoted some lyrics of a song I had written, called "Close your Eyes". Wow. Eddy confessed that when he had seen me, drenched in blue light, closing my eyes while singing, he had goose-bumps all over. "It transported me someplace else," he added. What a great compliment that was - someone seemed to "get me."

The second time we met, we bumped into each other at the local gym. I had just arrived at the club when I saw him going downstairs to change. "Awww, I just finished my work-out… damn! See you next time," he said. "See you next time," I responded with a smirk, waved and stepped on the treadmill.

About 15 minutes later, Eddy reappeared to my happy surprise and was blunt. He told me that he had already changed, but that he had a gut feeling about wanting to get to know me a little better and that the best way to get to know someone was to jog next to that person on a treadmill. I broke out in laughter. This guy was funny! He quickly added that talking would also help with not running too fast. His big, kind and innocent blue eyes made me smile - what an open and charming person had popped up in my life from out of nowhere. We jogged for 45 minutes, and we fell in love.

After this one treadmill conversation with Eddy, a simple, profound exchange of pure inspiration, respect, and kindness (!), I sat down and wrote a letter to Peter right after. Its content was short and straight: "Dear Peter, I have met someone. I have only talked once to this young man, and we knew more about each other and understood each other more than you and me in 4 years. I think you are a great guy, sometimes too rude, though – but you deserve the best, and I hope you find happiness. It is time for both of us to say goodbye and do what is right." That was the end of Peter and me. I had spoken my truth.

When I met Eddy, he was on a mission to change his life for the better: just like me! Eddy's goal was never to hurt anyone again. He had cheated on his last girlfriend, who had broken up with him because of that. There was finally someone who had learned a lesson and was trying to improve himself - how refreshing this was! I believed his guilt and thought he was trustworthy. To channel his negative emotions, he had thrown himself into a jogging routine, which was part of this reinvention. He also had just become a proud business-owner for the first time: About two months before I met him, he had opened a little store on the old fish market, right around the corner of my house: A skateboard, second-hand and home grow store.

Eddy was very much into legalizing Marijuana in Germany, but the centerpiece of the store was not related to pot, it was him. His charm, warm, kind and generous heart and his sweet and fun personality. Everybody came to visit HIM. He had turntables there, and all sorts of little funky and artsy gadgets and decorations.

Eddy's apartment was another extension of his personality: just like Tom Hanks' character's apartment in the movie "Big," Eddy's place resembled a living cartoon set full of funky toys and posters - a Peter Pan Paradise. He also happened to be the owner of the most wonderful and extensive LP collection I had ever seen in my life. Wherever Eddy was, there was music all day long. Our relationship was brimming with laughter, tenderness, openness, dance, and closeness abound. I was so utterly in love, and so was he.

But nothing is perfect. Eddy and I both had baggage that we brought along, too. At that time, both of us smoked far too much dope, and partied a lot. But at least we were working on our issues. Eddy told me about his trauma and trust issues related to being a divorce child. His father used to sleep around a lot, and so Eddy realized at the time that he had repeated his dad's pattern, as he saw the "same shit" happening with him. I was working on myself as well but was incapable of opening up about my darkest, most shameful secret - I still, as always, battled my daily bulimia. Nothing had changed. If at all, it had gotten worse.

The pay-off for being able to maintain a certain weight this way was long gone. It was only dreadful by then, disgusting, debilitating, and terrible. I most certainly would not want to tell Eddy.

I had missed the moment of opening up a long time ago. That's at least how I felt. I feared that he would lose respect for me because of keeping a secret like that and all my lies. I felt even worse because he had body image issues too and was always trying out new health regimes, like cutting out sugar and processed food. I never said a peep. I only mentioned that working out, as well as being fit and toned, was essential to me. I felt like such a sneaky hypocrite, having these heart-to-heart talks with Eddy about how important honesty, authenticity, and trust was for us, but all the while, I was lying and hiding my greatest demon away from him.

My parents didn't like Eddy, even though he was my first boyfriend, who adored my parents AND me. I always wondered why my dad had such an intense dislike for Eddy - Eddy was polite and respectful, he had an excellent taste, and knew a lot about design, which could have earned him plus points in my dad's books. But he also was the type of person who bought himself a glass plate, took some red bricks that he found on the street, and built himself a coffee table out of it. Eddy also used to store his colossal LP collection in old wooden fruit boxes. He put them sideways, stacked on top of each other, like a home-made bookshelf.

I recall my father once setting foot in Eddy's apartment, and how shocked my dad was after seeing that shelf. He must have thought that Eddy was a penniless bum. I was appalled by the thought that my dad would look down on people because of their finances. I remember getting angry with my dad for that.

I loved that Eddy cared for damaged, unwanted people and things in the same way that he cared for popular ones. People and things only needed to have a little bit of character to be worthy of his affection, no matter how old, cheap, and dirty they were. It warmed my heart and was quite contrary to how snobby and elitist I perceived my mum and dad to be at times.

I guess that in reality, my parents worried about how serious we were and how risky the outlook was for the two of us to end up married one day. I was only 19 at the time, and this relationship seemed to go steady. Maybe my dad felt threatened by another male in my life that had such a positive yet different influence in my life. Exactly that was what my father was so desperate for regaining.

The last Winter holidays before my finals come to mind when Eddy gave me an old and used treasure box on our first Christmas together. He had found it at a flea-market. My dad hated flea markets and "dusty old grandmother-stuff." The little box had the shape of a heart and was covered over and over with seashells. Inside was red satin, and I ADORED it. My parents and my brother, however, made sarcastic jokes about it all night long. They called it cheap and nasty and made it the running gag of the party, right in front of Eddy. Didn't my family realize that their daughter was happy for once? Didn't I deserve respect for myself and the guy I loved? I had tried hard to clean up my act. Eddy and I learned a lesson that night, as my family had hammered home that he was not good enough. Eddy forgave my family, but we decided to keep a distance from situations like this in the future.

Over time, I pretty much moved in with Eddy. I also got myself a job in a bar instead of getting hammered myself. I would still spend some nights at home and had my essential belongings there. My dad seemed okay with it, but my mother was more distrusting than ever because of the growing distance between us. But there were other contributing factors. During a fight, she yelled at me that she had opened one of my drawers that was overflowing with cash. I told her that I had no idea what she was insinuating. I always had HUGE tips and just didn't need the money for anything, so I just cleared out my pockets in there over a few weeks. She wouldn't tell me why that pile of notes was such a big reason for her sorrow. She probably thought I had become a drug dealer or a prostitute - I could only guess.

To negatively support my mum's worries, Cindy's mom, remember, a suicidal addict herself, had stopped her on the street and told her: "If you would only know what your daughter is up to behind your back. I promise you, you would turn around in your grave one day." The power of small-town rumors, paired with mental illness and lots of "broken-telephone-syndrome" – what can I say...

The last months of school were tough and riddled with some of the most memorable fights with my parents. A sad event had happened. Do you remember me mentioning my old classmate Ben before? The guy who was student president with me? Throughout the years, Ben and I had been in a theatre ensemble together, and we even dated for a brief period when we were younger, but it didn't work out, so we always stayed friends.

Ben, now 19 years old, just like me, had turned into a smart, adventurous, good-looking young man. I had known him for such a long time and felt close like a sister to him. He experienced a similar identity crisis to the one I had when I wanted to go to drama school, but his decision, despite his good grades, was to leave school and to become a carpenter. He was spiritual and a true Hippie at heart, all in all, a wonderful person.

Ben had been traveling and working on roofs around the world for a few months, and now he was back, wanting to get together for coffee. I was thrilled to see him.

When we met, Ben appeared to be a bit different – he was unusually energized and happy, when he rocked up at the bar where I worked to say hi. He looked different, extremely tanned, toned, and he also had long dreads now. After a few minutes of small talk, he told me that he had experienced a life-changing event: he had tried out acid. I only thought "I see… maybe that's why he is so different." But I wasn't concerned about him. Ben was lovely, very respectful of my relationship with Eddy, and I was genuinely happy that he was back in town.

Over the next two weeks, I saw Ben frequently. But my first gut instinct, the feeling that something was off, turned slowly into "a situation."

At first, I only noticed that the way he spoke became gradually more abstract. He would use unusual words and wanted to discuss weird topics, turning more and more into disconnected conspiracy monologues than coherent conversation. He also seemed to have lost a lot of weight in a short time and seemed euphoric about the tremendous amount of grass he smoked. He also bragged about how he didn't need to sleep anymore, and that he felt super-human. But worst of all: he just didn't stop talking! It felt as if he was drilling holes in my brain with all his rapid-fire monologues!

There was one particular evening when I had to ask him straight out to leave my home because the talking had gotten so intense that I felt dizzy and anxious. I had never asked someone to leave before, but I thought my head was exploding, and I also had to prepare for a crucial final exam the next day. Before Ben went, I made him promise that he would catch up on sleep.

The next day, after my test, I went to Eddy. It was early afternoon when the doorbell rang. We looked at each other in surprise because we didn't expect anyone. Suddenly someone outside started to shout my name. I looked through the window, and there he was: A topless, barefooted, smiling Ben, yelling "Hey, mama – I want food!".

Eddy and I looked at each other. My initial reaction was to laugh out loud, but Eddy knew right away that this was no laughing matter and said: "Let's better have a look at him, he seems strange?! Come on, let's try to get him up here, we should find out what's wrong with him."

By the time we were downstairs, Ben had vanished into thin air. Instead, Ben's mother and a doctor came running down the street, looking for him. They told us that Ben had thrown his glass-bong at his mother during some sort of a breakdown at home. Then he had walked barefoot through the shatters, as he screamed mad, esoteric nonsense, only to charge off right after with bleeding feet, no shoes and no shirt - just the way we had seen him a minute ago. His mum and the doctor had been looking for him for a few hours now. We decided together that Eddy and I should hold the fort there and keep Ben with us (just in case…), should come back. But nothing happened - no Ben. I decided to go home to my parents in case he would go over there.

When I arrived home, my parents were in a bad mood. I don't know if they had a fight or if it was because I had slept at Eddy's, or maybe I have never paid attention until this moment how THEY felt. Perhaps they simply had a bad day, too. I said hi, but got no response from either of them.

My father was in the middle of eating his lunch. He didn't even look up from his plate. Maybe it was the day my mother met the women who told her that she would turn around in her grave if she would know what I was up to, maybe something else, I don't know, but they were both in a terrible mood, as I said.

The phone rang just a few minutes after I had entered, and it was Ben's mother. She was extraordinarily calm as she explained how the police had caught Ben, running on the motorway, trying to stop cars. Since then, he had been hospitalized and "fixed," as in strapped onto a bed in a mental institution. Wow. Ben had gone crazy for real. He had gone mad, and I had been with him all the time without realizing it and without doing anything to help him.

He could have lost his life that day. I was terrified. I thought: If HE got mad, then I'll surely go crazy, too. We ticked similarly, and up until the day before this meltdown, I had understood every word of his spiritual, mystical Apache-speak rather. I turned pale and hung up after expressing my sympathies to his brave, strong mother. I was shaking and went to the kitchen and said: "Oh my God…" My father looked at me angrily and whispered aggressively though his teeth: "Be quiet. I need a time out, especially from you and your problems."

I didn't even let him finish his sentence and started to scream instead: "Ben is in a mental institution! And all you think about is your lunch?!!!"

My father's response was to grab the piece of meat on his plate and to throw it at me. It missed my head by an inch and left a big, fatty splodge on the white kitchen wall. I screamed. A storm of accusations thundered out of my mouth. How could he dare, how could he be so disrespectful, arrogant, and cold? The only thing that interested him was his bloody work or his design and his school! I was a person, and I had feelings! I was his daughter!!

The Hulk in me had awakened. I was so furious that I took him by his arms and got him up from the table. I opened the door of his office and threw him in. I had a force in me, I don't know how I did it, but it felt as if my dad, who weighs about 190 lbs, flew a few yards through the air. I shouted at him "Your stupid work! Go for it! And then enjoy your LUNCH!"

I slammed the door so hard that it felt as if the whole house shook for a moment. After that, I locked myself into the bathroom for about an hour. I could hear that my parents went out for a walk. I didn't feel sorry for my behavior – not a single bit. I hadn't been THAT violent, I hadn't thrown him onto the floor or anywhere else where I could have hurt him… I thought about our whole relationship and didn't know why we couldn't live together even though they were good parents. I knew that they loved me.

I short while later, I could hear the door again - they were coming home, urgh. I went into my room and waited, still upset about the news regarding Ben but a bit calmer. At the same time, I was still infuriated by my dad's cold and insensitive response.

Suddenly, there was a gentle knock on my door. It was my father, and I asked him to come in. He looked grumpy. I said "You know what? Not like that. My friend, you know him, BEN, has been hospitalized, do you understand? And you throw a piece of meat at me? Can you do anything else besides judging me and having prejudices about how bad I am? Have you forgotten that you have made me? Don't you think that there are similarities? Find them! I try, too. A BIG difference is that YOU have NEVER apologized to me, whereas I have to apologize for everything all the time - not this time. That's just NOT okay. If I cause trouble, I say at least sorry sooner or later. And I know when I hurt you. Go away with your angry face. There are sometimes more imperative factors in life."

Once again, I walked away and locked myself in the bathroom for another hour until I got hungry. The emotional distress had cost me so much energy that I had to get a bite to eat. In the kitchen, I met my dad. He was probably as hungry as I was. We looked at each other, and instantaneously, the anger was gone. He had taken my words in and admitted that I was right. He agreed that he indeed had never apologized ever for anything to me. He acknowledged that being there meant something else than being there as a watchdog. He had been there as a teacher, yes, but as a friend? He just didn't trust me anymore. He had even lost his belief in me. He had forgotten that I had a kind heart and that I was a smart person who knew what she was doing despite her rebellious acts. He had never sat down with me to ask me about my dreams and my hopes, and what I wanted.

That day turned out to be the turning point for the relationship with my parents. My father and I hugged for the first time since a long time, and slowly, slowly after that afternoon, I even became friends again with my mother, despite all the small-town rumors.

To follow through with action right away and implement change, my dad invited me out for dinner in the fanciest place in town, The Wallach-Hof. The Wallach-Hof was a decadent spa-hotel and restaurant where even our old chancellor Hemut Kohl would go to impress his guests.

I wondered why dad would pick such a place and why just he and I and not the whole family were going. Indeed, he had a hidden agenda and wanted to talk me into all sorts of things and had a ton of well-intentioned advice, but it all came out so wrong. He told me I shouldn't dye my hair black, that I used too much black eye-liner, that I should pick a decent study subject and not something artistic, and so on. But there was a lot of good that happened during this lunch, too.

It was probably the first time that I reacted calmly and appreciative, even if my father's words rubbed me the wrong way. Despite the fact that his ideas about how I should live my life wrecked on the shores of my thoughts, I understood that he was trying to be there for me. He wanted to be my advisor and mentor again. The tender bonds of a new friendship could develop from there, thanks to handling my thoughts calmly.

The next weeks were peaceful. Ben's stay at some horrible place in the countryside lasted longer than expected, and I decided to visit him. When we see situations like that depicted in movies, we may believe that the actors overdo it sometimes with their performances of being inmates in a mental ward. Unfortunately, they don't. The smell, the sounds, the dead eyes, the sadness there was real. People with scruffy hair, walking around with teddy bears in their nightgowns, some yelling, some screaming, some locked up, these places exist for real, and Ben was right in it. He had put on more than double the amount of what he had weighed before (!), and I almost didn't recognize him. His dreads had been shaved off, too. He was slow and drooled out of his mouth. When he cracked a joke about the dribble spot on his gown, we hugged.

Ben told me that his psychosis had been triggered by the LSD trip he had taken. According to his doctors, the combination of taking acid and grass had set off a spiral of severe chemical imbalances in his head.

The visit to a mental institution and seeing a close friend go through a breakdown like this, was life-changing for me in regards to my eating disorder.

I now had a glimpse of what a body that wasn't in a healthy balance could lead a person to become ultimately. Shaken to the core, I went to the library and began to study the human brain and researched what I was doing to my body chemistry with ketosis, bingeing, and purging. I only knew about the subtle, hormonal disturbances, my synapses, transmitters, and so on from school but not concerning mental or behavioral illnesses – especially not my own. I also considered for the first time to reach out for professional help.

Opening up towards Eddy should be the first step. Maybe, I could gather the courage to tell him, and perhaps he would not look down on me because of my sad, dark secret. I decided to wait and see. Eddy was not in the best place himself right now. He had financial problems, and we started to fight more and more. Keeping up my secret towards him was tricky, but I had gone for so long without telling him. How could I ever come back from this? How could I break the ice? The thought of disappointing him because I had hidden this for so long from him, scared me and instead of opening myself up a little, I withdrew more. I knew it was the wrong move but couldn't help it. I was too ashamed. I yelled at him, "Why don't we take a little break then, asshole?".

Eddy got so hurt that he, to my surprise and horror, called my bluff and added that we should take a step back to focus on our problems for a bit. He wanted to take care of his money problems, and I should concentrate on my A-Levels, i.e., the German version of graduation. Bulimia had won this round.

THE TAKE-OVER

~ A Sad Spring Awakening~

Eddy's and my little break turned into an on-and-off-relationship, and I found myself moving in and out of his apartment a couple of times during the next few months. Not very helpful for my graduation, i.e., my A-Levels.

And most certainly not for our health and well-being. Weed, alcohol, and parties were back in both of our lives – despite my research. I had concluded that I was a lost cause and already too damaged. During a particularly wild night out, I left him at a party after we had a big fight. I remember walking home for miles in high heels, drunk, angry, and ready to break up again. I was in the middle of my final exam that I had held out for OHHHHH! SO! LONG!

Also, my bulimia had reached yet another high-point - it had come back stronger than ever during the preparation period for my finals. By then, I had been battling bulimia for years. The energy I had drawn from it before, had now turned into feeling burnt out from the inside. Depletion and hopelessness had become the automatic setting for the day. That night, around 2 am, furious about Eddy, I stumbled into Eddy's home and decided to take that stupid pregnancy test that I had bought a few days before... Climax

. . .

Positive.

Time stood still. I stayed awake until Eddy came home. It was around 5 am when I heard a loud rumble and the sound of metal clunking and scratching, sounding like someone needed multiple attempts to find the keyhole. I had just stared at the wall - enveloped in darkness for hours.

Eddy was high as a kite from drugs and also heavily drunk. He fell onto the bed, still in his clothes, including his coat and shoes, and passed out immediately.

I screamed at him "I AM PREGNANT, ASSHOLE!". No response until the early morning. I had to wait until his alcohol-induced coma had worn off.

Right from the beginning of our relationship, Eddy and I had always talked about wanting to have babies together one day. I thought that he would be the father of my kids. He had already started to collect some items for "the little one," whenever he saw something special like tiny skater shoes or a special toy or book.

To cut a long story short, despite the hopes and dreams we had in the honeymoon phase of our relationship, and after a few painful weeks of thinking back and forth, we decided to move forward with an abortion.

I felt guilty. My period had been such a rare, almost non-existent event, that I had gotten sloppy with protecting myself during a few drunk nights with Eddy. I had convinced myself that I was infertile because of all the physical abuse I put my body through. A big mistake.

But as terrible as this experience was, nothing in life happens "just because." Not even an abortion. Pregnant, I experienced something completely new in my body: It was as if a foreign energy had taken over, and my bulimia had to move someplace else for the time being. It felt like being released from the prison of my addicted body when I suddenly experienced real cravings - these were natural, actual cravings, something that I hadn't felt for six years at least.

Hearing the voice of my body after the years of silence gave me hope for the first time, that my body might still be functioning after all.

Knowing that there might be hope for me was a silver lining that I never thought would be in sight again for the rest of my life. I had not destroyed myself despite the years of abuse. I stopped drinking and smoking, too. I HAD to. I simply was so grossed out by the smells that I couldn't do anything else but stop it. It was part of this re-discovered healthy dialogue with my body.

My new, unstoppable appetite, combined with my sensitive stomach, brought the vicious cycle of my eating disorder to an immediate halt. I was so intolerant towards junk food that I couldn't binge on unhealthy, sugary foods anymore – all I yearned for were healthy foods.

I believe that my vitamin-, mineral- and protein-levels must have been completely depleted. Anything healthy and loaded with nutrients was SO DELICIOUS. I hadn't thought of anything as "being delicious" for a long, long time. I had categorized food as bad (high in fat/sugar and calories) and good (zero calories) foods during the last four years, and the question had been "to obsess or not to obsess?" There had been no joy, only terror. And suddenly there it was again, the feeling of wholesome love and appreciation for the food I was eating.

The inability to make myself purge made me put on weight fast. Even if my diet was based on nutritious whole foods, my stomach muscles were so stretched out that I still had to eat a lot to be able to feel full and satisfied. My body was simply not used to keeping food inside anymore, and my digestion needed to re-adjust.

After a few weeks, I noticed that people began to tease me about "getting a little chubby," especially at my workplace at the bar.

At first, I was hyper concerned about how impossible my belly looked. But after a while, probably due to the hormones and the energy I derived from the healthy food, I was not outraged about myself and MY disgusting behavior, but about how mean other people could behave. Did they have nothing else to do than talk trash and make people feel bad about themselves? It was probably the first time in my life since bulimia that I made the choice not to give a rip about these kinds of people who made these types of comments.

Psychologically, this all in all tragic experience turned out to be a great revolution in my head. Especially because of all my exaggerated concerns about how I was coming across.

Being in control had caused me so much trouble throughout the years. Now here it was, my worst nightmare: people bullying me about my figure. But at that moment, when it happened worse than ever before, I realized that it didn't matter - I had bigger fish to fry. It felt freeing. I thought: "SO WHAT, M*THER-F-$%ERS!"

Pregnancy, even if aborted, changed not only my body chemistry but my perspective on life in general. It turned me into a different person. Forever. The impact that this rollercoaster of intense and mixed emotions had on me was rather profound. The gift that would stay with me even after the abortion was that I genuinely transformed into someone with a motherly outlook towards my fellow human beings - most importantly, also towards myself. I had escaped my own skin for a moment.

Once one feels life growing inside oneself, there is no way back from this again. The horizon has expanded. The baby I lost due to my incapability at the time, is behind this change of awareness. It remains. I apologize so very sincerely to you, little soul.

Life is about love, not abortions or eating disorders. Unfortunately, we learn these lessons through loss. The damage I experienced back then resurfaces over the years, and it will never go away. It is and stays a hole in my universe, an empty spot in my life. I accept my part in it.

Back then, pregnant and inconsolably sorry for having been so irresponsible and stupid, I still considered having the child until the morning of the abortion. Unfortunately, Eddy was extremely opposed to having a baby and kept on repeating himself: "We have to do this, as sad as it is." Eddy's main argument was that I had to live my life before we had a child. He saw the artist in me and confessed that imagining me to stay in our little town, working as a waitress, and getting old was his worst nightmare.

There were indeed artists who got stuck there down south, and we knew quite a few of them. Most of them had excessive drinking, drug, or sex habits. I knew that he was right in all these regards, but today I know that this was a short-sighted approach and only focused on the negative. The day came, and we went to the clinic. It was a heart-breaking day.

I went to Eddy's place after the procedure and spent the next few days there, sleeping, sleeping, and sleeping. I felt absolutely nothing. No guilt, no sadness, but also no relief - just nothing, if that's at all possible. But it wasn't like being dead inside, it felt more like numbness. The new 'entity' had left my body. Eddy and I smoked a lot of pot during this period and watched many, many movies. He on the bed - me, curled up on the sofa, not saying a word.

I was also done with school. Yes, I had been pregnant when I wrote my finals and had the abortion just before my graduation. My results were surprisingly good, but it didn't mean anything to me anymore. I went to the ceremony, disinterested and tired.

After a few days, life seemed to go back to normal. That's at least what we thought, but deep down, we so had not digested what just happened. I was in total denial, but behind the scenes, I developed a new nagging, dull, and ever-present guilt complex of being the murderer of my first child - a child with the man I loved. I guess we should have done some mourning work together. But we didn't. I bought a journal instead and tried to deal with what just happened.

About a month after the procedure, the first binge thoughts returned. I promised myself not to beat myself up when they began to knock on my door. Instead, I went deeper into the observer-mode. I tried to catch on paper, what was going on in my head.

Allowing whatever came up without being too harsh on myself was a fascinating process, and yes, the first binge came back, and so did the first binge-purge, until the old rhythm came back.

I tried to go with the flow and practiced to stay kind towards myself as I went through a relapse, followed by another relapse. During those, I would furiously jot down angry questions for God. I asked if he/she/it existed, why then was life so pointless on this planet? Why had he made me so weak and flawed, despite all my good intentions? Why had God, if God was love, allowed this pregnancy? Had this been a test, and I failed it? Was this terrible eating disorder my fair punishment for my wrong-doings?

The answers to these questions only came to me at a later point, when I didn't need to ask those questions anymore. How was I supposed to move on from here?

GOODBYE HOMETOWN – HELLO BERLIN!

~ Energy Never gets Lost ~

I spent more time with myself, still trying to digest the recent experience. I promised myself that I would try my hardest to make better choices in the future. And suddenly, I had a first tiny break-through with my bulimia.

I noticed that if I would value myself enough to take myself out to my favorite café in town to spend some quality me-time, I would not feel the urge to throw up, no matter what I ate. Sure, this wasn't cheap, but I embraced this new habit for a while.

For the first time, that real glimmer of hope was back and entered my eating disorder riddled universe. From then on, I would take a few hours a week to just sit somewhere at a beautiful café, bistro or restaurant, tucked away in a corner, all by myself. I would order, eat, and also keep my favorite breakfast in, while I was writing.

Poems and songs began to flow through me, switching to essays, truthfully contemplating what was going on in my head. I found many answers that surprised me.

Answers that had been stuck there deep within me. But as usual, the more responses I received, the more questions came with them too. This time, where I learned to enjoy spending time with myself, marked the beginning of a long journey that hasn't stopped ever since. I am that weird lady in a restaurant, sitting all by herself, smiling.

I cherished this self-soothing ritual so very much to this day and discovered many more ways to get into my happy space. Eddy, in a similar philosophical way, would venture out on a walk-about with himself for the first month after the abortion.

This time without the extensive use of weed, the crutch he would usually abuse for this kind of purpose. As a result, and more and more frequently, Eddy would sit down with me to talk about the future. He would say things like: "You HAVE to get out of here – now is the time, especially after what we have just been through. Don't stay here because of me. You had so many dreams when I met you - you always wanted to move to Berlin and to be an actress…"

I told Eddy repeatedly to shut up, because I loved him, and to make this discussion go away, I accepted a part in a two-person play in the little, but the cultured town that we called home. This play was my first professional job. It was well paid and guaranteed me union membership, health care, and pension benefits, the whole deal. Most importantly, though, my new job would quieten Eddy. But acting in my hometown wasn't a long-term solution.

After a short while, our phase of self-reflection died a slow and unglamorous death, and the pot-smoking and drinking came back. Sure enough, another round of full relapse on all levels washed over me. Spear-headed by my bulimia, despite all the journaling.

The time of deep poems, essays, and conclusions was over. I was so disappointed in myself. How could that break down again after everything I have just been through. Was this impossible to cure? Would I have to live with this forever? Was nothing sacred enough for me to finally teach me to stop this madness once and for all? Suddenly the last thing on my mind was spending time with myself. All I wanted was distraction from the recent past.

I also ignored all thoughts regarding the unknown future lurking around the corner. The fights with Eddy came back too. Splitting up had been dangling over our heads, but now there was a genuinely suffocating feeling in the mix. Eddy and I felt responsible for each other, even a little chained together by the recent sad event.

Co-dependency didn't make letting go any smoother. Eddy spent more and more time with other people. Women included, to my annoyance. First, his ex-girlfriend resurfaced, who just had a baby herself. I wasn't jealous per se, but the quality one-on-one-time he spent with her was something I was jealous of. I also didn't like the influence of other women in our relationship, especially not now. What we had just been through was something so painful and private, and I was horrified by the thought of Eddy divulging our intimate issues with a former lover.

When I dropped sarcastic comments in regards to his old female friends creeping out of the graveyards, Eddy went through the roof. As it goes in life, the more you fight something, the more you invite it into your life, and Eddy found himself a new female friend in addition to the old ones: Meet Verena, Eddy's new jogging partner.

Verena was a little older, and quite frankly, I couldn't stand her. She would turn up almost every day in Eddy's store, and bring him presents like cookies or gadgets related to jogging. When he told me about their plans to train for a marathon together, I freaked. Especially after all my open relationships, I knew how specific triggers could lead to more. "Oops, so sorry, it just happened," that was precisely my line that I had used too many times before. Worst of all was that I had contributed to this. Eddy and I had been jogging together as well, but ever since he started to train with her, I dropped out altogether. I was childish, probably, but I was somewhere else with my mind.

Verena was cold as a fish and fake towards me. I mean, come on, it was obvious what was going on. Well, for everyone but Eddy. In the beginning, I tried to avoid Verena entirely because I couldn't play her pretentious game in return. I was worried about getting into a fight with her.

I was certain, that if Verena and I were longer than a minute in a room together, I would drop a sarcastic comment or even tell her that it was evident to me that she was trying to snatch my boyfriend. I just KNEW she wanted to start something with Eddy so badly. It was written all over her behaviour - the way she looked at him, and how she played that game that women put on when they are keen on someone. Like, when girls agree to EVERYTHING, the guy says so enthusiastically and when they like everything the guy likes so enthusiastically, too. When they giggle all the time and twirl their hair while bending their neck slightly sideways and start to subtly touch the guy all the time and always smile, smile, smile… Urgh! She was older, desperate, and prepared to wait until I had moved to Berlin. I knew this "best buddy tactic," and the patience that women are prepared to invest, well. I was an expert at it, having used the same scheme with David.

My gut instinct was right. Much later, Eddy told me that Verena had casually asked him during that time if he wanted to have a baby with her. Not a relationship, no, "only" a baby. Right. After we had just been through an abortion, which she knew of. Verena explained to Eddy that it was "getting late" for her and that he would be "perfect" as a "donor." She would care for the baby "all by herself." Ummm… yes. Sure. First of all, how would the baby get in there? Not via artificial channels and second, by having a baby with Eddy, she would chain him forever onto herself, because there was no way that Eddy wouldn't show up as a dad. How sneaky. Why didn't she just go to the sperm bank?

Eddy didn't agree to this crazy deal, but he told me that he had considered it for a while – gulp! I didn't blame Eddy. He was not switched on in the mature relationship department. Remember, he had been a child of divorce, and had never lived or experienced relationship longevity. He just had been trapped like a naïve little fly in a sneaky Venus trap, that's all.

So, there we go. All this happened right in front of my eyes. But when I tried to voice my concerns and warned Eddy about what his "jogging-buddy" was doing, I got mocked as "being jealous." I found that insulting since she had, in my eyes, not much going for her. Neither did I find her attractive, smart, nor exciting in any way, but I guess Eddy needed the attention to boost his ego.

Eddy's new female friends weren't the only problems, though. I had gained a few pounds again, and the first awful comments got under my skin because the weight I had put on would not go down. Gone were the pregnancy hormones that had helped me not too long ago to shrug those comments off in anger. There was, for example, one of my new colleagues from the bar, Helen.

She was a beautiful, yet undoubtedly anorexic woman, who would talk the whole day about nothing but dieting and how " she thought she was. One day, Helen pulled me to the side in the kitchen and told me that my boss, who I once had turned down as a prospective lover, by the way, would say horrible things about me in front of guests and staff. She elaborated on how he complained about me being an embarrassment and showing my new fat belly around.

Today, I am not sure about Helen's true intentions for telling me these comments in that way. ANYWAY, what matters, is that I felt terrible about myself and started the ultimate diet with total restriction. This was my first long anorexic phase. I would show everyone how much I could control myself if I wanted to!

What was I thinking? I started a liquid diet with buttermilk and juices, and the weight would indeed just fall off of me. I felt as if I was on a total high. And after a few months, I missed the social meals and the feeling of a "good old binge session."

And then I had a thought that never occurred to me before: how immensely powerful the combination of extreme restriction PLUS bingeing and purging could be! I only ever tried one or the other. This new technique was so easy and effective! I even managed to reduce the amounts of food I would binge on. I felt my stomach shrinking, and then my body followed. Finally, for the first time, a diet had worked. I felt as good as I hadn't in a long time physically, but mentally, I had arrived in crazy-land.

My every thought was consumed by diet, calories, restricting, looking in the mirror, checking, weighing myself 25 times a day, there was no time for anything else, and nobody knew, as always. To the outside, I seemed "perfect," like I had never been before. I even got on with my parents.

Everyone showered me with compliments - even my colleagues from the theatre and Eddy congratulated me on how great I looked. These positive comments were the fuel I was living off. This was all I cared about - until I found myself breaking out in tears on a regular basis. Do you remember the story about the lady, the croissant, and the perfect latte? That's what I'm talking about.

At one point, I broke down crying at home after a massive binge and purge that had come unexpectedly. I had starved myself for days because I was trying to become purely anorexic and failed. I heard my mum come home and frantically tried to clean up the mess, but my eyes were so swollen, and my face was so puffy that I looked terrible. I washed my face with cold water, but nothing helped. These eyes were here to stay for a little bit.

I unlocked the bathroom door and tried to sneak past my mum, but she saw me and asked if I was alright. "Everything is totally shite," was my reply. And then I cried again. My mum asked me if I had issues with Eddy, and I replied that that was the least of my concerns. "I think I have to move away from here, mum, this town is killing me," slipped out of my mouth. My mum was a little overwhelmed but hugged me and agreed that it was probably time to "leave the nest."

Going to Berlin was my only chance to find sanity. There was no chance for me to not run into trigger after trigger after trigger. I had to re-build myself, if I wanted to save myself from this f&^$*ing disease.

Acting-wise, there was nothing that I could do here beyond what I had already accomplished. I regretted that I hadn't left school the day I had that chat with the headmaster and that I had only focused on Eddy and our relationship.

The day came when I started to send out my resume and headshot to drama schools, but I did it half-heartedly. I felt far too old (I was 21 by then, isn't that ridiculous…), and I was truly tired out from the dark struggles in my life. I was also scared of leaving the only person I trusted, my Eddy, but what can you do. I knew that he couldn't come with me. Not for the next couple of years, at least. His life had become quite problematic since he had started his business. Eddy had lost his driver's license on his way home from a trip to Amsterdam because he and his partner had forgotten a joint in the glove department, and the border control had found it on their way back to Germany. In addition to that, there was another problem: Eddy had a business partner, Erkan. Erkan was selling so-called "scented pillows" filled with magic mushrooms if you know what I mean. There was a legal loophole at the time that had made it somehow legally possible, or at least not legally forbidden, to sell or own mushrooms if they weren't intended for consumption, i.e., disguised as a "scented pillow." Complicated thing.

To keep this short: One day, the police came and confiscated them. The two boys argued with the police and explained the legal situation, but the police was not in the least impressed. It was a big scandal in our hometown and landed in the newspaper. People weren't that happy anymore to give their children money to buy their skateboards, clothes, or other items in Eddy's shop. The costs for a lawyer regarding their drivers' licenses put a drain on them, and they even worried if they would end up in jail. This scandal enhanced Eddy's bad self-image immensely. He already had always felt that he wasn't good enough for me. Knowing that he was the main reason for me to stay behind was making him feel guilty, too. And now he was the dodgy-drug-dude in town.

Eddy made me promise that I would finish up with my theatre season and then move to Berlin the following spring. From there, I had to swear that I would apply to drama schools. Now, all Eddy and I could do, was try to enjoy the last six months together to the max.

Even Verena had to bite the bullet. She got extremely upset about Eddy telling her straight that she was asking him for too much of his time that he would instead want to spend with me. I didn't even care anymore at this point. Funny that problems stop to exist once we stop kicking up a fuss about them. Oh, sweet, sweet justice.

The excitement in regards to planning a big move got me a little bit out of my depression. But I wanted Eddy to be happy, too. We were not only lovers but also best friends. How would he cope without me in his current mess? I at least would have a whole new universe to conquer, but he would be stuck here even worse than I had ever been.

Having reached this kind of deep level in a relationship, although it was time to move on to the next chapter, gave me finally courage to open up about my secret. I didn't tell him that I had bulimia or anorexia, but that I wasn't looking as happy inside as I came across from the outside and that I had a secret that I was keeping from him. I dared to move a tiny step further and explained that losing some weight had come with a high cost and that I was a little worried about my mental sanity sometimes.

Eddy reacted scared and sad, and responded, to my surprise, with a confession, too. He told me that he used to be a fatty when he was little and when his parents were fighting, he would lock himself in his room to eat two packages of sugary cereals to throw it up afterward. In other words: Eddy seemed to have his OWN experience with bulimia. We never talked about it after that.

I probably should have taken the opportunity to say what was up with me and ask him for help, but it was too big of a step and awkward since it was still happening in my life. I didn't want to burden him with putting this on his shoulders, as well. Especially not after the abortion and just before taking off. Eddy had been the best boyfriend I could have wished for, the one who had shown me what it means to love and be loved.

Eddy had brought so many gifts into my life. He truly inspired me to find my inner child again, which I had abandoned for so many years. Eddy also had sharpened my eyes in regards to living a natural, eco-friendly life during our two-year relationship. He also inspired me to take a more active stance in protecting our planet. Eddy's activist interests also lead us both to find out about pesticides and added food chemicals, and what they do to your body.

Before I met Eddy, I had only focused on calories. I couldn't care less about chemicals or GMOs. As an "a-few-times-a-day-bulimic," nothing had mattered in this world. I was a mad person who did something horrible, unhealthy, and disgusting on a daily basis that was far worse than pesticides on my apple. Why should I care about chemicals in the food that I would throw up anyways? But Eddy got through to me with patience, love, and kindness and inspired me to watch out for chemicals and toxins.

Another great gift that I received from Eddy in this department was that he cured me from being hooked to artificial sweeteners. Before I met Eddy, my favorite sweetener was a zero-calorie liquid that came in a bottle. I put it on everything. On the label, it said, "use three drops for a cup of tea." I probably used the equivalent of 50 drops, but I wouldn't stick to one cup of tea, I used to drink tea in jugs and needed to buy a 500 ml bottle of sweetener about once every week. Eddy had to work hard on me about that. He explained the same facts to me over and over. I just didn't want to hear any of it for a long time. I thought that I knew it all better. When I was in my anorexic phase, I felt that no one could understand what better to eat and what not to eat than me. Even when Eddy told me that artificial sweeteners are used to fatten up animals, I thought to myself: "Well, I'm not an animal, and I can control myself. Sweetener helps me because I need so much of it in everything. What about using real sugar? Or honey? Are you kidding? Oh, no, I would become "fat" again. No way."

I have a feeling that some of you might know this love for artificial sweeteners or diet sodas. And isn't it also interesting to take notice of the fact that when "normal" people try to give you some advice about your body, diet, and health, it feels as if they don't have a clue, right? But oh wonder, thanks to the power of love, Eddy's approach got to me after a while. The day came, when I promised Eddy that I would stop with the sweeteners once and for all. His method to convince me had been sweeter than any aspartame, saccharin or sucralose could ever be. He would come to me to show me cut outs of magazine articles, and books. He inspired me to learn a lot about food altogether.

As a result of learning more about natural ways of living, like sticking to an organic diet, I also stopped dividing food-groups into good and bad groups. I was still a long way away from beating my bulimia, though, because I hadn't worked on my emotional problems. As a result, I got obsessed with that new healthy lifestyle instead, and I had to welcome a new demon into the ring: exercise addiction.

Before, I had always enjoyed working out, but now I would spend hours and hours in the gym. When I got sick, however, and my new sacred routine crumbled, I felt so guilty about not working out, that I fell back into the old habits.

Excessive binges would go on for weeks, and I would eat and eat and would throw up and up and up. I had been so disappointed about myself throwing up again. Now that I finally had reached skinny-land, now that I had my A-levels, a part in a play, gotten over the abortion, and having smartened up about the meaning of a healthy diet plan.

It had been a constant battle backward and forwards, where the main subject of my problems was the need to be in control. Why do we always want control? We don't have it anyways. We have to die one day. That's some loss of power, isn't it? What sense did it make to become a famous actress? What sense did it make to travel the world, to write scripts or books, to make movies, to experience adventures, to have friends, or even have children, only to lose them in the end?

But one day towards the very end of our time in my hometown, Eddy would also take my fear of death away from me. We had one of our conversations about the meaning of life, where Eddy asked me what I thought about death.

I told him: "Well, let's not kid ourselves here. I am still working on my belief in God, but when it comes to death, even if I'm trying to stay open-minded, I honestly don't know. But it is probably oblivion. The End, Game over."

Eddy thought a while about my statement before he answered that he didn't believe that at all. I must add here, that Eddy had never been baptized or brought up with any other religious belief, so I was surprised. I asked him to be a bit more specific about his ideas regarding death. He looked at me in that way that made me melt, with his blue Peter Pan eyes, those kind, wise and innocent eyes: "I think," he said, "that, for example, what you and I have CAN'T get lost. I have no clue what happens, but in physics, energy never gets lost. Nothing just disappears. We are probably going to end up as two beams of light dancing around each other, somewhere in space."

That was the best thought I've ever heard. My life had just changed. "Energy never gets lost."

Suddenly I noticed that there was so much more to life than what I had thought. Was God peeking through the veil again?

A week later, I stumbled over a story about a Buddhist monk and a cup of tea. Someone asked him about death. He dropped the cup and said: "Look." The person with the question said: "Oh …it's gone." The monk took a cloth and cleaned the floor, held it up, and said: "It's here." The person said: "but the half got into the earth, and you will rinse that cloth."

The monk said: "Tea is always tea." Well, I guess that is what Eddy had been trying to explain to me. Tea is always tea. Energy could never get lost. It could only transform into new forms of energy. The possibility of a continuation after death made me wonder. Where, for example, other wasted energies would go if they would not disappear. Where would our tears go and our pain? Suddenly there were so many questions again!

It probably DID somehow make sense to be here… it MADE sense that we have something like a conscience that tells us what is right and wrong. We KNOW that it is terrible to kill, that we shouldn't lie, steal, and be nasty to ourselves or others. I knew deep down, that I was a GOOD person and that it wasn't ME who was deliberately being awful, to binge and puke, to lie and insult myself. But where did it come from?

I was open again. Open, to receive answers to questions that the agnostic heart I had at the time, would have blindly answered with "nothing." But I would make sure to stay away from any religion. Instead, I promised myself to become a listener to my heart, trying to understand its language again. God was a subject that I didn't want to think through too fast. It was too vast and overwhelming. That whole death-energy thing was enough as a next step forward on my spiritual journey for now.

When I tried to analyze and journal about my ED and the epiphanies resulting from looking at the past, I was impressed and wondered what would happen if I would investigate my surroundings in this fashion. Were there causes from the outside that I could eliminate?

There was indeed more to having an eating disorder than just a f#$%ed up me. This eating disorder was a complicated thing, and I became determined to find out everything that had ever been said or written about it. "I want and will get rid of it. There MUST be a way" is what I thought. "I got myself in it, and I will get OUT of it!" If spirituality could come back into my life, maybe, one day I would be able to come back from this, too.

Whoever I was, I wanted to like myself again, which needed to be the first step despite my eating disorder. If Eddy could love me, I couldn't be SUCH a horrible person to get along with. I realized for the first time that I was sick in the sense of having CAUGHT something, not something I DID to myself.

I felt some new wind beneath my wings. I went ahead with putting my move to Berlin into the last steps of action, even if it meant that Eddy and I had to say goodbye soon. Our love would simply transform into something new.

Getting my belongings together that I wanted to take to Berlin with me had significant and exciting momentum. I also put a beautiful little book collection together for my first weeks in the capital and picked some out about Buddhism and Yoga. I was ready to go.

Eddy and I had kept the ending open until then, but the night before we loaded my things in a huge truck, we decided to let each other go completely. We broke up. Lovingly and mutually. Not being with each other would hurt us more than allowing the other person to be with someone else.

We felt like angels for one another and knew that we would love each other forever and ever because of this great sacrifice. It hurt tremendously, but there was so much love that we proved the words wisdom about loving and letting go. With Eddy, I had found so much: Thanks to him, I had regained a positive and happy, sometimes even CHILDISH attitude because I HAD LOVED and felt LOVED in return. It was so good to know that I was NOT the notoriously horrible person, a cheat, liar, and cold as a fish as I had believed about myself.

The opposite was the case. I had found my values and principals again.

But unfortunately, with eating disorders, even if you humble yourself and get down on your knees, pleading with the universe for this to stop, once you are ready in your mind, it doesn't work like this right away. There is no instant fix because wanting instant fixes all the time is what we need to overcome. Making a firm decision is only the BEGINNING of a PROCESS that needs to be PUT INTO ACTION after the realization has been reached.

Let's all be grateful for positive angels in our lives for a moment. I firmly believe that you are having a few positive people around you, too. They are the ones to stay close to. I know, their positive attitude might sometimes be like salt in an open wound if you cannot bear to be too close to someone genuinely positive. If that is the case, start with practicing gratitude in a small way. Like saying thank you to your body for simply breathing, or for the sunshine or whatever it is that makes it easy to be grateful.

172

The'practice of feeling gratitude will grow into a healthy part of your life. Open it up for the supporters around you. I had just left mine back then, ready to try out how I would handle life being by myself in Berlin.

The excitement about my first week in this fantastic new city and living in my first own apartment in Berlin kept me going without missing Eddy. I felt amazing. I also had taken on a neat job in one of the best and hottest restaurants in town, where the celebrities would go to. Only seven waiters worked there, and it was quite a privilege.

David had been responsible for this. He had moved to Berlin a year before me. Vibes were good between us, and I was reaping the benefits of our old deep bond in this phase of my life. He, just like me, had escaped from our home town, too. Randomly, he had met the owner of this famous restaurant about a year ago, and he offered him an apprenticeship as a cook. So only living for a week in this great city, I already had an apartment in a great location and this crazy job with these exciting guests.

My eating disorder was dormant in the first month. I only dieted because I had put on a little weight because of not purging, but all in all, I was proud of myself and believed that this might be the end of it.

Cooking for myself most definitely helped a lot with not wanting to throw it up, but instead of using food as my drug, I instantly became a queen of the night again, just as I had always been in my hometown. This time, however, everything was bigger, better, faster, higher. I would spend all the money I made in the restaurant in Berlin's night clubs. Partying, drinking, and smoking pot was all I did. My party behavior spiraled out of control to the point where I would wake up every day at 12 with a hangover and a lung that made me feel like a 70-year-old chain smoker.

I felt guilty, unhealthy, and alone and dreamt every night of Eddy. In addition to the home- and heart-sickness, I also had a bad experience with my hair.

I always cut my own hair, but this time something had gone wrong. Can you imagine what happens when you try to get it straight, and you cut off more and more until you find yourself looking like a broomstick upside down. Well, that happened to me.

Out of frustration, I decided to start a new diet. A radical one was needed. Now that there was no one else to monitor me, I could probably succeed for the first time ONGOING, now that I could shop and eat without anyone seducing me to eat bad stuff. I began by eating only oranges for a few days.

To my despair, I didn't lose a single pound and was only bloated and starving for five days. I didn't know why I didn't lose weight, only that I felt horrible. I had enough. Shaking, I put on a hat to cover my shitty hair-job, put on some unwashed pants, and ventured out on a big shopping trip. I feverishly ate everything up, and it ended, as usual, in the toilet. Bulimia had arrived in Berlin and came back stronger than ever before.

In the next months, I would spend all my money on it. This time I was anonymous in a big city, and there indeed was no one that could stop me. I found myself crying one night, crying out loud for Eddy. I realized that I didn't want to be without him. I felt an insatiable hole in my stomach, and the only thought that calmed me down was him. I didn't call, though. Thank the heavens that he did! It was like in the twilight zone.

Eddy was in a bad state, too. He cried on the phone and told me that he was pacing up and down his apartment and that he experienced physical pain because he missed me so much. We had to come up with a plan!

The first time he came to my place in Berlin, I sat down with him and told him about the horrible last month and that I was worried about losing my marbles. I added that I had severe mental health issues and that I believed I was an addict, heading toward a fate like Ben's. Eddy looked scared and hugged me. He asked me if I wanted to explain my troubles a bit further, but I declined. He suggested that I could move in together with someone, but I couldn't imagine that at all. What about a pet? I needed a buddy, a pal, someone that would be happy when I come home, someone to hug and to care for.

I didn't know about the therapeutic effect of furry friends, but the idea felt right. We didn't wait on it and bought two tiny little rabbits, and I named them Peace and Joy. And best of all, we decided to be a couple again, even if it meant that we needed to lead a long-distance relationship for an unknown time.

After a few days, Eddy had to go back, but I felt a lot better. Two months went by, and I tried my best to decrease the shopping trips and not purge by any means. I drew strength from having confided a little bit in Eddy, and I didn't want to put myself into the position where I would need to tell him that I was doing worse.

Out of the blue, the call came that would turn my world upside down once again: Eddy told me how much he loved and missed me and that he wanted to give it the best shot ever with me by giving up his shop so he could move to Berlin and start a new life with me. I was thrilled beyond words. It was like a dream come true.

TO LOVE MEANS TO BE ABLE TO LET GO...

~ Broken Glass for Christmas ~

The first month of living together was magical. My eating disorder had disappeared entirely. I even thought that the moment when Eddy moved in with me, and we had each other again, that it was over for good!

But one cannot base one's happiness on someone else, and the reality would catch up with us sooner than we could count to three.

To get out of his business, Eddy had bought himself out of his store-ownership. Unfortunately, he also had taken up a steep high-interest loan to pay for it. His partner had been quite happy about that in the beginning, but two months later, Eddy found out that he was incapable of managing the shop all by himself. In the past, Eddy had done EVERYTHING, and Erkan had no clue about the work that was involved in keeping a store afloat.

Calls kept on coming from people telling us that the guy would not even open the shop! Eddy started to get more and more worried because he still owned half of the inventory that needed to sell, so he could keep up with his monthly loan payments. Erkan didn't seem to be concerned, though, and we heard more horror stories through the grapevine about Erkan spending all his money on cocaine. In the end, he disappeared until the shop got closed for good by the authorities, and the debt collectors had confiscated all inventory.

In addition to Eddy's continued financial disasters, the trial related to the mushroom pillows was lying ahead. The legal costs would eat up an additional small fortune. Hardship came upon us, and my earnings were just enough to feed us. Eddy, slowly but surely, started to slither into passive-aggressive behavior. After a while, I understood the underlying message: he blamed me for his financial situation.

It started with little "remarks." Not loud or overtly aggressive, but mean. Eddy would say things like that I was greedy. I was shocked! Why would he believe I had the money to pay for these bills? If I had it, I would have put it down in a heart-beat, but I didn't. Maybe Eddy thought that my family was wealthy? Was this MY responsibility? Doubt crept in if I, indeed, WAS a greedy person. Eddy couldn't understand that I didn't even offer to go into minus realms to help him. Out of insecurity, wondering, if I was not supportive enough, I went to my bank. I had never used my overdraft. I never needed to. After my appointment with the teller, my bank account would always be in overdraft, up to the maximum allowance.

The fights about finances affected us on many levels, and we also stopped making love. The pets started to annoy him too, and the apartment was suddenly too small for his taste. Petty, unimportant issues suddenly drove him up the wall. On top of his problems, his sister caused him heartache as well. She was a year younger and smoked ten times as much pot as we did. Debt collectors were also knocking on HER door. She was caught up in a relationship with an ex-con who had just been sentenced to go back to jail. To help her out, I suggested that she should move to Berlin to live together with us. She loved the idea, and we moved into a new and much bigger apartment.

At that time, my bulimia would only come to me when I was alone, so the concept of a crowded house sounded perfect for my situation. Cooking all meals for all of us gave me a good structure, and I noticed that structure helped me. The place we had found was fantastic, a massive apartment in an old house in all in the art-nouveau-style with high ceilings, wooden floors, and a princess tower. The rent was just about the same price that I had paid for the small place.

We all agreed that I would be the primary tenant on the lease and that Eddy and his sister would give me their contributions. I took the lion share, though, because I was the only one who had a decent job.

When the apartment was still empty, I went in by myself, all excited, and hung up a picture. Eddy got so cross with me for doing that and scolded me. He told me that this was now also his place and that I had to ask before I decorated. Oops.

We were different now, meaner, more desperate, and most definitely irrational at times. It had a lot to do with not making love anymore. The more we tried to talk about THAT subject, the more complicated it got. He blamed me, and I accused him. It was mainly him, though. He was caught in a maze of frustration. He applied for one job after another, and always got fired after a month or so. This pattern seemed to be circular. A new job, getting fired, then he would stay two weeks at home, smoke weed all day, and be depressed, and then he got a new job again.

I, on the contrary, got tired of waiting to make my dream come true, so I finally started to apply for other drama schools. I had missed the annual audition at that specific school that I wanted to go to so badly because I felt that I didn't have the time to prepare. But in fact, I had been scared to fail. I had wasted my time trying to make ends meet, cook, and care for Eddy and his sister, almost like a mother. The efforts that went into giving them the feeling that we were a family and also to save money, made me forget about my eating disorder and my doubts and worries for a moment. It was a distraction at the time, but most certainly not a long-term solution.

When I got into a drama conservatory about two months later, Eddy pulled me down from my cloud 9: He told me that we couldn't go on like that and that he wanted to move out. I couldn't believe what he'd just said - after the hardships we've been through! After all the love, and promises, after everything! He DID move out, and I had to stay behind with his sister because I couldn't cover the rent all by myself. I was in shock.

As soon as Eddy had moved out, his sister told me that he had met another girl at work. When I asked him questions like if there was someone else, he vehemently denied it until we broke up over the phone. My world had broken down.

What a blessing drama school was. At least in that department, I was on my way. However, another anorexic phase began. I had worked out an incredibly strict ultra-low-calorie meal plan. In combination with the dance and exercise classes, we could take advantage of at school, I finally looked acceptable, according to my old diaries. I was thin as a rake to be precise. Way too thin. I became very irritable, and my blood sugar levels were consistently low.

Christmas was coming up, and I decided to stay alone in Berlin while his sister went home to the little hometown down south. I had loved Eddy so much and simply couldn't imagine looking in my parents' eyes without continually breaking out in tears. Everything could have been so perfect. Through the Berlin ex-pat community, I had found out that Eddy wasn't going back either, so both of us spent the first Christmas alone and separated in the same city...

I was unable to console myself. Christmas Eve approached, and the city had become empty. Snowflakes danced their way down on the grey and slushy streets where the odd car would drive by in a hurry to make it to the dinner table among friends and family. To my surprise, as it slowly turned dark outside, there was a strange feeling of peace instead of devastation.

I wanted to try and treat myself. It was almost as if I had accepted that in the end, all I had in this world was myself when it came to it. To honor this new friendship with myself, I cooked myself a four-course meal.

Before I finished my appetizer, I called home and opened the presents my parents had sent to me. They were sweet and thoughtful. Among them was a bottle of champagne to mark this first Christmas away from home as a special one.

Once I hung up, the quietness came back - this time mixed with a pinch of unease. I turned on my favorite music and proceeded with the cooking, but then I made a mistake: I began to drink. First, the whole bottle of champagne and afterward, and then, I opened a bottle of red wine. Drunk, I broke down and started to cry my eyes out.

I cried and cried so much until my face began to swell up. After the loud howling sounds that I had started with, lasting for 30 minutes or so, I embarked on cry phase 2, a mopey, self-pity party, where I just went over and over how betrayed and helpless I felt, mumbling out loud to myself. As the tears were still rolling down my cheeks and nose tip, I turned on the television. They were showing "Gone with the Wind," which I had never watched before. It turned out to be EXACTLY the wrong film at the wrong time. The howling returned. This time, feelings of fury bubbled up. And then I did it. I called Eddy.

He sounded distant and instantly picked up on the fact that I was drunk. I didn't beat around the bush and blasted a stream of insults at him right away. I accused him of quickly finishing off with me to start with that girl from work. I screamed at him that he could shove his promise to never to betray again up his behind.

He hung up, and I threw my glass against the wall, screaming and stomping my feet on the ground. I kicked the wall and threw a chair until I fell onto my bed and in a deep and angry sleep.

When I woke up, everything was just as bad. But on top of it, my head felt as if it had been put in a blender. This Boxing Day morning blues would stay with me for months on end.

My instant reaction to this meltdown was to have one affair after the next. I was ruthless. I took home whomever I wanted to, but, of course, instead of feeling better, I felt worse. I even slept with David after all those years. The morning after the one-night stand with him, I woke up to a massive hangover. When I realized who was lying next to me, I felt awkward and empty inside. I also noticed that I had lost my purse with all credit cards in it.

I looked around and reached for my glasses. All my plants had died overnight too. The day before, they had been fine, but that morning, they were looking terrible and were wilted and dried out. It was a spooky feeling, and I decided not to repeat sleeping with David ever again.

More flings and one-night-stands with other people would follow. I just didn't know what to do with myself, but thank God, this time, there was also a steady bright light in my life: drama school.

Going to school kept me busy all day. I had the time of my life there. And despite yet another personal crisis, I seemed to be stable to some degree with my bulimia. I was in that kind of limbo-state that I described at the beginning of this book. This is what many might confuse with the final stage of recovery - when you feel you are disciplined and manage your condition, but you are still scared of a sudden, unexpected relapse. Food is still not enjoyable, and you can only follow a particular diet consisting of safe foods.

Remember, this is NOT full recovery yet! Inner freedom, and joy when you eat and cook is complete healing - do not settle for less! I didn't, and we are almost there - just stick with me a little longer, beloved reader.

The problems with my other addictions weren't also solved just yet. My sex and party life had become my new method of choice to cope with my pain. It wasn't about sex, though.

Many times, nothing happened with the guys I took home. I sometimes just wanted to be with someone and needed the feeling of being hugged.

At other times, I needed to know that I was still a hot chick after having lived the life of a cooking mama for the last year and a half, taking care of Eddy and his sis.

Speaking of her, Eddy's sister finally also wanted to move out. It started with her going on and on complaining about the rabbits leaving their little droppings everywhere when I let them out their cages. I always cleaned up after they were out, but that wasn't good enough for her. According to her, the rabbits were supposed to keep their poop inside their butts or stay in their cages.

A month later, she moved out as well, and I was all by myself again in that fabulous apartment with two vacant rooms. Would I manage without relapse?

CRISIS-CHRIS

~ Single, White, Female ~

Knowing myself, I knew I put myself at risk of relapse by living by myself. I didn't want to slip.

I got active, and for the first time, I and patted myself on the back for seeking preventative measures. A new roommate was needed, and there she was: Chris, a girl from school.

Chris was tiny. Length and weight wise. She had short hair and a cute face, but she looked more like a 12-year-old boy than a girl. I thought she was sweet, but everyone kept her at a distance. Later on, I would find out why.

To me, Chris seemed alright as a person but not exactly a good actress. Her main issue was that she overthought every movement on stage, and in general, she was too full of doubts and problems. It killed her playfulness. I would spend a lot of time trying to build up her confidence. I truly had a soft spot for her. I guess because I was impressed with her courage because Chris was communicating that she was an anorexic in recovery. That impressed me - still, I wouldn't dream of confiding in her, or even of making my problems public as she did.

After a month of living together, I noticed that she would not just openly, but also ALWAYS talk about anorexia. Her constant urge to overshare didn't come across as normal to me anymore - this was obsessive. How much could a person talk about it?! Connected to that, the other thing she just kept on telling everyone, if they were interested or not, was that she had a milk and sugar allergy. The third, most irritating compulsive subject of chit-chat, was that she interjected wherever she could, what a good Christian she was. Supposedly, she would never lie. "I am just so honest, that's my only mistake." How often she used this sentence!

Next, Chris started this whole phase of suspecting a few girls from school to be anorexic. She would urge me to talk to some teachers about them because she claimed that they wouldn't believe her because of her past. Needless to say, I didn't speak to the teachers, but boy, would Chris put the pressure on.

The situation grew a little awkward at home. I started to smell my perfume in the hallway. "That's okay," I thought, "friends can use my things," - but it would be nice if they'd ask. I went and asked Chris if she had used it, knowing that she just DID because I could smell it.

Instead of admitting the obvious, Chris broke out in a fury! I was taken aback. It was OBVIOUS that she had used it. I had bought into her whole "I'm so honest"-thing and then this reaction?!

This clash of realities bugged me, and I wanted to put her to the test: I placed my perfumes and creams in the bathroom in perfect order. I put them precisely, I mean EXACTLY in a particular position, for example in line with a tile ridge or labels pointing exactly straight in one direction, so that I could immediately see if she had used my things or not. She did - most of them.

I sat down with her and confessed in an amicable way that I had put out traps and that I knew that she used some of my belongings. I added that I wouldn't mind if she used my possessions at all, but that she shouldn't lie about it. She denied it again. This time, Chris burst out in tears, but she was STILL denying it and got cross with me. I gave up arguing about this. Now I thought that this was plain silly. Why bother about this "stupid little" thing - a few drops of perfume - no big deal.

But then, some more strange occurrences happened. My diaries and drawers were subject to further tests, and I prepped them with small secret traps to see if she would touch them, as well. Indeed, she would read all of my journals and snoop through all my drawers when I wasn't home – sounds somehow flattering? No - it was sad and scary.

Besides the matter that Chris was using or snooping through my belongings, I also got suspicious of her trying to play mind and power-games with me as one of her latest quirks.

Already just after moving in, she had started to buy sweets for me, that she couldn't eat herself because of her "allergy."

I told Chris that I didn't want chocolate or other sweets for myself, but she bought them again and again for me as presents. I pleaded with her to stop it. I confessed that I would eat the whole jar if there's chocolate spread at home and that I would eat the entire package of cookies, too. She wouldn't stop buying them. I confronted her more directly and inquired why she would buy me foods that I didn't want to have or eat. I humbly confessed that I was "a little bit" addicted to them.

The next day, as if we never had the conversation, she had brought a new packet of cookies home and put them in my cupboard. I ate them and told her again: "Please do not buy me cookies or sweets! You see: I can't resist!"

The next day, she put some chocolate mousse in my cupboard. I still thought that she was sweet, maybe she was just a little stubborn and obnoxious, and so I ate it. I tried to talk to her one more time: "and please, no chocolate hazelnut spread, either! I can't resist, and I don't want to gobble all of this up."

One day she would give it a break, but the next day the chocolate mousse would rock up in my section of the pantry shelf again.

I got angry this time and threw it away. The next time, she would bring cookies again. The penny dropped. She tried to play games with me. It sounds odd, I know. I couldn't believe it either in the beginning.

Once I had become suspicious, I noticed more and more. Some of my sexy underwear went missing. What was Chris doing with it, if she took it?

Life at home with her started to feel spooky. I remember getting worried for the first time about my safety when I had a male visitor in my room after a night out.

I could hear her footsteps in the middle of the night, coming towards my door. She opened it with a low, squeaky sound. I told the guy to act as if he was asleep, and we waited. She looked at us for a long time. Parts of our naked bodies were sticking out from under the blanket, and we almost broke out in laughter, but we were to creeped out.

From that night on, I started to lock my door at night. The facts added up. I wondered if I was crazy or if she was nuts.

One night we had another fall-out. It was about something at school, as usual. I advised Chris outright that she would have to develop a thicker skin. I added that she needed to stop the complaints and that she had to show strength instead. In response to the advice she had just asked me for, she suddenly got mad at me and pointed with her finger in my face, screaming, as big crocodile tears gushed from her eyes: "You are so cruel! I wish this would happen to YOU!"

That now made ME angry for a change. I had invested hours and hours and hours of listening to this chick, trying to help her. I put my foot down. This was the last time I would ever talk to her about school.

Without a word, Chris got up, and grabbed her purse and shoes to leave the house - without wiping her tearful face. She seemed to want to keep her tears stuck there to her cheek like a creepy decoration to show the whole world what I had done to her.

At that moment, the doorbell rang: It was Miriam, another friend from school. Miriam was beautiful and a "Berlin girl" - born, and raised in this cool place, and she was every inch as cool and magical, as her city. I liked and adored her very much. She was smart, fun, and so talented.

As Chris left, accompanied by a loud gasp, Miriam entered and asked me what was going on. Thank goodness there was somebody who I could share all the mad little details like the perfume, underwear, and the door at night with.

Miriam looked at me for a long time. Finally, she would break her long, thoughtful gaze at me. Miriam put it straight and told me that she couldn't understand how I could have moved in with Chris in the first place. Everyone at school was wondering about this little girl's mental stability. Her eating disorder talk and the boys' underwear she had been wearing hadn't gone unnoticed.

Miriam and I opened a bottle of beer, smoked a cigarette, and wondered what to do. I confessed that I had doubts about my own sanity and how grateful I was for her giving me a second opinion. Miriam only gave me that long look once more took another deep drag on her cigarette, and said: "...You really have no clue, do you? Do you know how wonderful you are? The opposite is the case, honey. You are not hard; you are too soft! You always try to see the best in people. Do you know how many people adore you, and how many more are jealous of you? Believe me. If you have any "problem" at all, it is that you sometimes see good where there is none. I'm telling you, Annie, there's something wrong with Chris. Not with you."

I was very touched. Never before had a girl said something like that to me. Miriam looked at me, and I looked at her, and we decided to search Chris's room for my missing underwear and CD's. We needed to see what was going on in my place.

What we found was shocking. Chris had stolen my sexy underwear and had sewn it to her size. Nonetheless, that discovery was harmless in comparison to the next. Enemas, laxatives, and diet pills were scattered everywhere under her mattress, where she had stashed all her 'treasures' away.

We also discovered hundreds of little coffee creamers that had all been sucked out empty through tiny holes. And of course, there were around 10 empty jars of chocolate mousse and cookie wrappers, too.

Chris had been bingeing and hoarding, and her allergy was a total lie. Everything that this little girl's mouth had been promoting about herself, had been a big bunch of lies.

Miriam's next discovery was boxes and boxes of hair dye in the color that I usually dyed my hair in. Chris had never dyed her hair ever?! Why store a hoarder's load of my hair coloring? It was spooky how someone was able to deceive everyone by proclaiming to stand for truth and recovery so loudly. I, who had been a compulsive liar too, had an extra hard time to wrap my brain around it. There was something psychotic about this stealth of a copy-cat, and her snooping behavior, and theft.

The story with Chris ended with me asking her to move out, and she left school shortly after that, as well. I put in my own one month notice for the 'wonderful apartment,' that had seen many of my troubles, too. Every corner reminded me of the past, anyways.

I distinctly recall one of the last evenings in that apartment, again on my own. I was in the bathtub. Most of my belongings were already packed in boxes and ready to go wherever I would find a new place. I had lit a few tea-lights as the apartment with the French doors, and the princess tower slowly turned dark. I watched the sun disappear behind the milky glass as scenes kept on playing back in my mind, and I found myself in a sad place.

I wondered what would have happened if I had said or done things differently. Would Eddy and I still be together? Could I have done anything to avoid all of this? Should I have given him more reassurance? I moved on to other melancholy themes and suddenly thought of home, the small town with the cobbled streets and the cathedral and my family, that I loved so much. I thought about how quickly time passes, and that every time I saw my parents, they had gotten a new grey hair.

I thought about my mother and tried to imagine how she had given birth to me. I tried to imagine how it had been for her to be pregnant with me, to see me grow up, those worries when I didn't come home. I missed her. I wanted to tell her how much I loved her. In my family, we never really said "I love you" with words. I only noticed this fact at that very moment. But it was okay. We said it in different ways, and I knew I was loved.

I wondered if my parents were really happy with each other and about how little I knew about their lives in general. I asked myself for the first time if they had fulfilled all their dreams and hopes, and then, suddenly, out of the blue, I knew I had cut an invisible umbilical cord, tying me to them. Zzzzzing...

It was time to let go of a few other things, too. There I was. Alone, all one, no one left from the old life, on the right track regarding my education and despite my broken heart, my own shoulder to lean on. Just at this moment, life had sent me Miriam. She became my best friend ever since. I never knew how essential it was to have a female friend with whom you can be just the way you are. You can cry, you can make mistakes, you can be silly. It doesn't matter because you know that person loves you, respects you, and will always forgive you and vice versa.

Since meeting Miriam, 20+ years have passed. A few select other friends of a similar caliber followed, and I am a blessed person to know these beautiful people.

Through finding true friendship, an artistic home, and my faith in God, my belief in justice and love grew back stronger than ever before, too. I even managed to make real, lasting peace with my parents. This time, however, all these new opportunities were not inspired by a new guy or relationship. No.

All of my new-found joy had been created by me and blossomed through my commitment. I discovered that it wasn't bad at all to be with myself if I just took good care of myself.

The less I went out drinking and smoking, the less trouble I caused, and there was suddenly nothing to feel guilty about anymore.

I realized how important it is to be surrounded by only kind, genuine, and positive people. Finding good people is not as difficult as I had always thought. Once you have found the place where you want to be, you'll be yourself. This way, you meet the like-minded folks. The rest consists of learning how to listen to your heart when it comes to others: the ones that do you good and make you feel good ARE good for you.

Based on these new conclusions. I wondered if I should try to get back together with Eddy. He had done so much good for me. Was he still my dream guy?

I called him to see how he was doing. He was so happy to hear from me, and just by the tone of his voice, I knew that it hadn't worked out with his crush from work.

After all these years, I had deciphered our relationship pattern, and if I would not be desperate or clingy, he surely would ask me out. I was right.

Eddy took me out on a few romantic dates, and it was apparent that he wanted me back. He confessed that he had missed me, and we discussed if we should get back together again.

To my own surprise, however, I, against my usual impulsive behavior, thought that I would like to take some time to think about that.

Stopping myself from a passionate yes was something I had never done before when it came to relationships.

I gave myself a week to wrap my mind around Eddy and me, weighing all the good feelings for him against all the negative feelings I had experienced during our relationship. We had gone too far. I noticed a big grey cloud in our relationship that always left me feeling sad. Feeling this sadness out a little further, I dared to take a look into the future, something you can only find in your heart too - nowhere else. There was none for us. I just knew it.

Unfortunately, it became crystal clear that there was no chance of maintaining a friendship either. I knew that as long as I met Eddy now and then as a best male friend with that extra sparkle dust between us, the chemistry that would never go away for life, I would not be able to meet another man, either. To love another man like I loved Eddy would be impossible. How could someone else possibly have a chance? My inner clarity turned into an irreversible choice.

I called Eddy, and we met up at a lake. I asked him, after the saddest hug in the world, to never contact me again. I loved him, and he loved me, and this time we had to let go of each other forever - sadly, also, as friends.

That was the hardest goodbye a person could go through. It's like someone died. It is tough to stop all contact with someone who was the center of your universe. We had been crucial for each other's lives, but the time was over. I would have never been able to listen to the stories about his future new girlfriends, and I wouldn't have wanted to tell him about my future husband, either.

You think that this is nonsense and that one CAN be friends with an ex-partner? Fair enough, but I simply couldn't, as I was a freshly awakened, sensitive, raw baby being, just in the process of learning how to walk again. Eddy was someone with a key to my heart. He was able to open it in an instant, by merely looking into my eyes. We've made love many times, so he also knew how I smelled, how I looked, and how I behaved in these intimate moments.

If you meet a person that you shared intimacy with, memories pop up in the head, let's be honest, even if it's only for seconds. I didn't want to share these private thoughts with anyone else than the person I'm committed to.

Ironically, the lesson that was now hurting Eddy, I had learned from Eddy himself through his friendships with his ex-girlfriends. It had driven me crazy. They were there with 'support and advice,' as soon as we fought. They knew a part of him that I could never understand. I did not want to join these ranks and be that person in someone else's life. It was a sacrifice, but I never regretted it.

Only sometimes I would get a bit frightened or sad over the years. I imagined what would be if I would find out that Eddy was dead or unhappy because I had let him down.

Analyzing my feelings for Eddy more critically, I noticed that I suffered from some kind of Samaritan. A VITAL piece of self-discovery! Do you make other people's problems YOUR problems? Have you ever tried to "heal" anyone by making up for everything they have been through by trying extra hard? This is not, how a relationship should be, especially not a partnership.

How deeply love can connect. But it was the right choice to remain separated and start again with a blank slate.

But I was not yet at that stage where I had played enough with fire, and I had burned enough, too. Not only myself, though.

The initial phase after this final split with Eddy turned into a phase of drifting from one guy to the next. I can't explain to you how sorry I feel about having hurt a lot of men. I've been mainly talking about relationships, but I had so many affairs too. Most of them ended brutally. I always thought that if I'd be just honest and admit upfront that I didn't want a relationship, I was playing fair, but that's not the way it works. It wasn't fair. I left these poor chaps open, took their hearts out, and scrunched them. Some of the guys hoped that once I started seeing them, they would get 'through' to me.

There is a strange principle that human beings always want what they know they can't have. It makes closed off people like I was way more attractive than they are. Some of the poor guys wanted to prove to me that I only didn't want a relationship because I couldn't see who THEY were.

Some kind guys tried to help me, because they sensed that I had gotten hurt in the past. Then they would give me a little space, while I would go out with another guy and move on. After breaking it off with one particularly sweet guy, who had showered me with gifts, love, and attention, but I was just not interested in anything long-lasting, I had another mirror moment.

Had I turned into a liar and a bully again? Sure, it felt good to be desired and not to be alone, and just to snap my fingers and a young man would try to please me, but it was all based on a lie.

I had talked myself into believing that it was okay to "just have a little fun," but looking in the eyes of my last sweet affair, who felt shattered, wasn't fun at all. It was cruel and pointless.

Why was I not more responsible with others, if I knew that I had no serious interest? Was this a gender thing? A role reversal? Was I getting back at David, Stefan, and Peter?

I put the break on love affairs and remembered the state that Eddy was in when we first met, where he had made a pact not to hurt anyone anymore. I took time off to think about my behavior. Nothing good could ever come from fooling around with guys - only heartbreak.

Taking an honest self-assessment in terms of my failed relationships, I noticed that the black spiral concerning my personal relationships had a similar face to that of my eating disorder. If I wanted to get ready again for a new serious relationship, I concluded that first and foremost, I needed to make sure not to fall for a person where I subconsciously wanted to work off my guilt.

I did not want to get trapped again in the circle of suffering and hurt as a result of not analyzing my feelings before I chose my actions and partners. From now on, I wanted to make conscious, PRO-LIFE, and PRO-HAPPINESS choices.

The penny dropped: that was the moment when I realized that all addictions and obsessions have a familiar pattern. My relationships, over-sexuality (i.e., "slutty" behavior), excessive partying, and negative self-talk, mirrored my eating disorder throughout the years.

There was a direct link here, and the commonalities I noticed were as follows: when repetitive patterns of negative behavior started, I would not want to think through the effects of my actions in their entirety. I would only be looking at the short-term solutions, the instant fix. I would only look at the fastest and easiest way to help me over that "bad stretch," that "one lonely night", that need of losing "those five pounds," that stood between myself and perfection.

It was a "Eureka-moment." I told myself "Annie, here is what you will be doing from now on: as soon as you start something that feels off, something that you don't want, something that negatively affects you or others, STOP! Where is this going to lead to, Annie? Tell me ONE positive outcome. A little bit of admiration? Gratification? Can't we just wait until we meet someone who we like and want to be with? Like… for good? Or are you scared to pick the wrong person again, Annie? And don't you want to experience this happily after feeling between you and you? Can you please make peace with your body, mind, and soul, be forgiving, patient, kind and make a pact never to let yourself down?" Good question. Why didn't I just pick the right person instead of playing hunting games for my ego? Why wasn't I always my own best friend? Why wasn't I able to?

Another epiphany occurred to me: Most of the time, when I made my bad picks with guys, I was DRUNK or at least tipsy or fell for flattery.

I also noticed that every excessive behavior resulted directly in a lousy self-image. The very same thing that had caused me to look for love outside of myself!

What if I would would put my full focus on only giving myself and others support, instead of negative self-talk? I related this theory to food and how I treated my body: What if I would only do and eat what I loved and what made me feel nourished, satisfied, and proud of myself? I had never seen what a full-on addict for many different and unhealthy substances and behaviors I was.

So far, I had considered drinking, smoking, drugs, and sex as harmless and normal behaviours. Loving to hang out at clubs until the crack of dawn and just being a bit wild, was not harming me. Or was it? Wasn't the cute sounding label of "partying," okay to experience? Wasn't I just "having a good time?" Sure. But I reached the conclusion that there was nothing good about it, if it ended in lousy health, negative self-image, and bad relationships. I had confused "doing what I want" with "rebellion," and I always thought that escaping meant to be "free." This was not being free - this was the opposite! Having zero limits, and no parameters was, in fact, being chained.

Freedom means to be able to make happy and healthy choices and to help yourself. Freedom is not to look away and make excuses, as we practice acts of compulsively damaging ourselves when life challenges us. I've had my fair share and more of these hazardous and damaging escape mechanisms for this lifetime.

After many years of self-punishment, I had finally concluded that anything excessive, eventually leads to problems that are likewise extreme. I was finally willing to give up feeling bad about myself for good – in all areas: as a daughter, a friend, a student, a woman, a partner, the owner and operator of the divine gift of my body, and as a child of God.

MY LAST TIME THROWING UP

~ The Sweetest Experiment of All ~

Spring break was coming up, and I had moved out of the old "haunted" princess tower home.

Planning to go back home for a 3-week vacay to decompress before going on a new round of apartment hunting in Berlin, I was looking for a holiday home for my bunnies. I found a family who lived in a house with a large garden.

When I returned, the kids cried so hard when I wanted to take Peace and Joy back, and I gave them away. I knew that even if I loved them to bits, we were ALL happier if they were in nature with these doting kids.

It was not easy to say goodbye to my furry therapists - especially one rabbit was close to my heart. She was more like a dog and would jump on my leg when I called her to snuggle when I felt down, but freedom and grass were a better retirement place for two bunnies than wherever I would move on to. I already had received so much love from these two fluff-balls, and it was time for them to bless another family.

All excess furniture and clothes were gone, too. I wanted to keep it light and moved in the apartment of a friend from work whose contract I was taking over. I spent the first time in my new tiny place, just laying low, thinking about my plans, hopes, desires, in a calm and self-loving way. What a great practice this was. During this reflective and reclusive three-month period, I knew that I, with all of my heart, didn't want to ever again binge and purge. Instead, I made a deal with myself.

I knew that through the process of taking everything in my life apart so I could learn from it, I would discover many unpleasant things that I had done. There were memories, I had buried there. I promised myself that I would consciously practice to not beat myself up about anything, no matter what painful moment from the past I would re-visit. I wanted to find every unhealthy pattern that was left.

Giving myself this blanket-allowance to be kind and generous to myself, I noticed, to my surprise, that there was not that there were not many prisons left on my list to escape from.

This way of practicing to look at myself with love and forgiveness only, INCLUDING my eating disorder, was working. I noticed that the anxiety of confronting things that were uncomfortable to look at had decreased over the years. I noticed that I had stopped judging myself. And amazingly enough, through that, I stopped judging others. Stefan, William, Peter, Cindy, David, Mr. Oxblood, all these people were merely people, fighting their own battles.

There was no need to hold on to grudges anymore. Only forgiveness and a humorous perspective were left. The people mentioned above had contributed significant punchlines to the story of my life. They were teachers, not correctional officers. I was the one who had all the pieces to my freedom stored in my heart.

I could see so much clearer now, without any hidden agendas. A significant portion related to my eating disorder was dedicated to my "teacher," Chris. The lecture she had given me was in buying me those sweets that I compulsively binged on when they were in the house, not knowing how to stop myself.

Thanks to Chris, I became aware of the fact, that I needed to look into trigger foods that I had still been bingeing and purging here and there. I discovered that the leading trigger foods were sweet. I either would need to stay away from these types of trigger foods altogether, or I would have to eat a whole pack of whatever it was.

I decided that I didn't want this kind of abstinence. I wanted the ultimate freedom because I LOVED cake, chocolate mousse, and cookies, and I wanted to be able to eat a normal amount with others or by myself if I wanted to. I wanted a COMPLETE return to health and joy when it came to food, not a contained version.

Why exactly were sweets my greatest challenge, and not crisps or burgers? I figured that there must be a psychological reason for this, not a physical one since I was eating enough carbohydrates again, so a carb deprivation could not be the cause.

I asked myself "Annie, what is going through your head when you want to binge?" And then I did some sort of a method acting exercise to explore it. In therapy btw, as I found out many years later when I went undercover in various treatment centers, there is a similar technique called "psycho-drama." The method acting technique I used worked like this: I first relaxed and then put myself in the headspace of a real situation that I had experienced. I allowed the feelings and thoughts to come back, and then I put them in words.

When I did this exercise, I was astounded by how many different types of voices there were in my head. I tried to pick them apart by writing everything down.

Lines popped up in my head that were as old as my childhood. That was the moment when I had the revelation of the existence of "shitsdoms": Sentences that my granny had dropped crept out of my sub-consciousness, like the "fat hand"- comment when she set me on a diet. I noticed that despite her concerns about my figure, she always used to express her love with sweets because she wasn't able to hug, or kiss much. My dad must have had a similar experience as grandma Kari's son. And that was something that had been transferred from dad to me. What a ripple effect this was!

Going back to the source, my granny, I wrote down in my journal what kind of treats and desserts she would give me as a reward and a sign of affection, and there was quite a variety. There were also memories of fighting over treats with my brother, when the two of us got going like two hawks fighting over a mouse, ripping the bag apart and trying to grab as many gummy-bears as possible. (As an adult, I smirk and wonder where on earth the supervision was - laugh out loud!)

Memories of finding my parents' secret hiding places in the house where they kept the forbidden and expensive Belgium chocolate came to mind.

Wow, this was the beginning of deception, lying, and stealing as a child. I always used to take piece by piece, feeling annoyed with them and self-righteous, because they wouldn't share the good stuff with us kids. Weren't we good enough for Belgium chocolate?

I wrote down all of the brands and the types of sweets that I thought I never got enough of, including the famous chocolate mousse. I created a list of all the sweets, treats, drinks, and desserts that I had always WANTED but hadn't been allowed to have. During that process, an ingenious thought popped up in my mind: what would happen if I would buy all this? What if I'd buy so much of it that I would not be able to binge and purge everything in a week, or better: not even in a month?

My inner scientist did what science suggests when there is a question bothering your mind: I put it to the test.

I went to the bank, withdrew around 400 Dollars, and began the most fantastic shopping tour that one could imagine - my empty cupboards at the new place needed to be filled! It was mad: I bought not only one of each type of candy. Instead, I purchased packets and packets of them.

The cashier looked at me as if I was either crazy or as if I had a children's party coming up for the whole neighborhood. She probably had never seen someone with a cart like this. Neither had I! I filled up all my cabinets, especially a piece of furniture that I had brought from my hometown and had belonged to my sweet gran Mimi. I put what I considered the best treats in that kitchen cabinet. What I had bought should have lasted me for weeks, even if I would binge on it every day.

Interestingly, I didn't feel inspired to eat anything from my hoard at all on the first day. On the second day, in the evening, I started to open the first bag of gummy bears. Then I opened some chocolate and a box of pralines. I didn't binge, but I indulged. It was a funny feeling to have so much of something that you couldn't run out of it, even if you try - that fact in itself made it almost impossible to binge.

After a few days, the sugary treats almost started to taste and feel a little boring - I knew that I had found the solution here. I ate my way through tons of treats and sweets in the next weeks. I ate them like they were regular food, with a calm, disciplined attitude as if I was running a marathon. Towards the end of my experiment, I even began to feel a little sick just by looking at them. My compulsive sweet-tooth pattern had dissolved for good.

The whole experiment ended almost in a comedic way. I had put on about 5 pounds during my weeks of the sugar-craze - no big deal. I remember this one, specific last time purging as if it happened just yesterday – and I didn't even binge! I just wanted to get rid of this disgusting sweet and sticky food inside me because I knew what an awful headache it would give to me. I purged - something that I hadn't done in a long time.

As I had promised to myself, I wasn't going to be upset or disgusted about myself, and I also wasn't disappointed. I just looked at the chocolate-dough-textured substance in the toilet bowl and started to laugh.

For the first time, I felt a natural relief after a purge: I knew at that moment that that was my last time ever to purge food.

Until this very day, that is the fact and will stay a fact until I die. Today, I still enjoy chocolate or a cookie, a piece of birthday cake or a pastry now and then. Otherwise, I have fruit and a flavored yogurt or tea with honey, but that's pretty much it with sugar - no cravings, no deprivation, ever since. I'm just over it - thanks to this "exercise." There is nothing that can make me go back. I know too much.

I have experienced all that there is to experience without getting damaged more severely. I have cavities and don't know if I will develop early osteoporosis. I had an iodine deficiency for a long time, and so on. But all in all, I walked out with a very livable existence, compared to collapsing dead over a toilet bowl because of a brain hemorrhage or a heart attack.

HAPPY END

~ How to make Deals with the Universe ~

This final time of throwing up gave me wings to fly. With the newly found confidence that anything was possible, I quit my job as a waitress. I didn't have a clue how I was going to finance myself, but I prayed and asked the Universe to help me.

It might sound short-sighted and impulsive, and not exactly like what I had promised myself, but I DID think things through.

I analyzed again, and found out, that if I continued to work so many hours in a job that I so did not want to do, all my energy would be put in negative emotions about this job and not transformed into positive energy towards achieving my goals. I declared clearly to myself and the Universe, that from now on, I wanted to earn money with my real work: with being an actress and an artist.

Intuitively, I knew that everything would turn out alright, no matter how scary giving up that financial security would be. It was logical. And it got frightening.

I lost my apartment and couldn't pay my bills and temporarily moved in with Miriam. Miriam only had a tiny studio (!), and we would live together for three months. She was a true angel, and we had a great time. Within these three months, many things would fall into place - The Universe delivered, and I got discovered by one of my favorite directors in Germany.

It was like in a fairy tale. Not only did I get my first television lead role, but I also earned my first 10,000 bucks. During this time, I also fell in love with the camera guy, but hold your horses - it didn't work out. Yet again, another lesson for me.

It left me, as heart-aches always did, in pieces, despite all this new energy and magic. I asked myself, "Why? Why, oh, why did this kind of stuff still happen to me? I thought that I was on the right path now! Why wasn't it streamlined and easy now? Hadn't I found the "recipe" to live a happy and fulfilled life now? It had worked with my job and eating disorder, why didn't this work with love?"

The answer surfaced in moments of silence. I finally allowed myself to listen deeply within without being scared: THERE IS NO RECIPE FOR ANYTHING. All that there is, is constant growth if you always try your best and show respect. All you need is a great attitude, while you keep on having your own back.

With that as an inner compass, life, instead of being predictable and boring becomes more game of rolling with the punches. Life is not supposed to be perfect. Instead, it presents us with ever-new challenges to allow us to grow as happy and prosperous as we want to be.

So why did I have to experience heartache again, with this camera-guy? What was the message? I had promised not to screw around half-heartedly anymore, wasn't that enough? Indeed. I noticed, that I had fallen in love according to yet another pattern that I should be breaking, instead of reacting to.

After my successful candy experiment, i.e., the last time I threw up, I also wanted to clearly define what kind of partner I wanted. I was done with meaningless encounters.

I knew I was ready for a stable relationship, but a thorough examination of what was right for me was necessary. If I had a catalog to order a partner from to suit my personality, what would a partner for life need to bring to the table? "Please, dear universe, do not send me another actor!" were my first thoughts when I sat down, trying to define what Mr. Right would translate to in character traits. I was sure that I wouldn't be able to stand a fellow actor long term. I felt I had enough passion for this profession in my life – another person in love with the job like I was, and I would go insane.

To my surprise, I also found out that I needed to separate work from private in its entirety, going forward. That's why it hadn't worked out with the camera guy. The lines were too blurred in this business for my taste. At school, we had the motto "Don't f%^& the company" as part of our professional code of ethics, and it made perfect sense to me after I had burned my fingers too often.

I prayed and contemplated again, as I had done when I quit being a waitress, asking the Universe to bring me acting work. This time I asked to meet my Mr. Right based on my list. I asked God to help me not to develop a crush on the next best handsome person, but instead, TO BE PICKED by someone. By a stable, healthy, happy person with a golden heart that stands with both feet on the ground, ready to commit to me all the way. I vowed that I would not even kiss a man if I couldn't envision marrying this person. I didn't care how long it would take. I would stay focused on myself and on being the best person I could be until that, what was right for me, would manifest.

When my husband ran after me to stop me on a steep flight of stairs about nine months later, he simply swept me off my feet with his huge, kind heart, and we decided to get engaged after three days.

Our story gets better, the older we get. In the beginning, many people thought we were crazy, but time proved that when you know who you are and provide for yourself what you need to be happy, God delivers. That was now 16+ years ago. I love this angel that got sent to me so much. We traveled a lot and moved to London, then to New York, where I started this book, and now we live in Los Angeles, where we currently own and operate a production company together. But most importantly, we are the proudest parents of the most beautiful, smart, healthy, fun, and kind-hearted children.

Bulimia didn't stop because I bought a lot of sweets one day. It ended because I filled the hole in me with being me, letting my problems go and by making conscious, healthy, long-term choices.

I stopped myself from feeling guilty and from feeling sorry for my parents, for myself, and the rest of the world. I was able to end this unhealthy habit because I opened myself up and allowed myself to be vulnerable.

That brought not only the right kind of friends, mentors, job opportunities to me, but also my life partner. I learned how to end the nightmare of having an eating disorder for good by achieving the ability to tell others and myself that I loved them.

It stopped through me being able to freely say, "I love you," without blushing and MEANING those words, and through having friends that can tell me, without shame, that they love me. These friends are my family of choice. And yes, most importantly, finding and loving myself no matter what I do is the skeleton key.

And of course, I don't get it always right, but I still have only kindness, sympathy, and understanding for myself when I fail.

Wanting to be happy has always scared me. In my "lab coat", based on my many years of study, I dare to present to you the thesis that the ability to hold happiness is the last outer layer of addiction. It is the type of relapse that hits you like a bullet in the back. When we haven't consciously embraced happiness, we don't believe we DESERVE IT. Or we fear that striving for bliss is pointless because supposedly all good things have to come to an end - another "shitsdom," we have been told. But remember, if you dare to believe in a potential realm beyond this physical dimension and you remember that energy never gets lost, you can create your own reality. We just need to think on a much higher level and not a small, mundane and earthly one.

Pursuing happiness without duty or purpose had always felt selfish to me in the past. I have changed my mind about that. Now I know that I can only give from the point of inner abundance. And that means that I have to put my well-being first. From that overflowing well of health and strength, I can share my happiness with every living creature on earth.

The people who see that in me and who give back, stay around automatically. It is a beautiful natural process. It is like an automatic "crème-de-là-crème-magnetism." Contrarily, I now can also allow people that receive a red-flag from me to wander off, never to see them again without feeling bad for them. If people are ONLY concerned about themselves and try to "sell you" their self-centered points of view, if they are disrespectful, negative, and complain a lot without searching for solutions, I know that they're still kind of "sleeping." I don't want to disturb them during their snooze.

There are also no "holy grounds (at least, when there are other Human beings involved)," clubs, or communities that guarantee a person's integrity. The film industry is spiked with vain and self-centered people, but there are also incredibly inspiring and kind visionaries, too.

It is the unexpected places that deserve extra attention when we are screening our environments. We need to look extra carefully, where people are supposed to be "good," like in church or charities.

A wolf in sheep's clothing is the most dangerous one because he gets close to us and uses our trust. A particularly well-disguised toxic person manifested itself for me in later years in the eating disorder recovery scene. The person turned out to be one of the biggest suckers of my time, creative energies, and heart-blood. This person had caught me right off guard in this community, that means so much to me. This person got his/her "fangs" into my neck because I naively assumed that being a survivor of this disease means that we are all automatically united as sisters and brothers. So even though this person felt off to me, I followed my old "Samaritan" auto-pilot, the one that turns a blind eye to damaged people that take without giving back. I put my "vampire-detector" aside - big mistake.

You see, the learning never stops, and I am sure that I will meet more teachers until the day I die. And also, for this person, I have only gratitude left.

I learned from this experience how to protect my intellectual property, to keep written track-records and witnesses around, instead of relying on verbal agreements - especially when it comes to business. It was an invaluable lesson for a trusting person like me. Sure, it hurt, and I felt betrayed at first. But once I noticed the changes I need to make and implement, the pain ended.

Only gratitude for the received knowledge remains. When it comes to finding a suitable environment, a trustworthy friend, a mentor, or a lover, we always need to double-check with every individual we meet.

We need to ask ourselves if we feel anxious or inspired, respected, and whole in their presence. Be it a fellow sufferer, be it a therapist, or someone in another sacred space like church, school, or family. Do you FEEL BETTER when you are with them, or do you notice question marks, or feel exhausted, or have a pit in your stomach?

I do not condemn, or "scratch" those energy-vampires off of my list of "worthy" people, though. We are all worthy. But I don't spend time with people who feel off to me if I don't have to. It's just not helpful for them or myself.

People that affect you negatively can be like little black holes. I get thrown off balance. ME helping THEM back to embrace love, gratitude, forgiveness, peace, and the process of constant growth is a one-way street. Sadly, most of the time, they are not even aware of what they are doing.

On the positive side, it is interesting how effortlessly the right kind of people find each other if they stop trying too hard. The wrong type of person simply falls away. There is an abundance of happiness coming from just being yourself. What a gift it is to stop being DESPERATE. Not having to be liked by everyone, and not having to prove anything to anyone anymore is blissful freedom.

How awesome it is just to BE. I don't have to do anything special. I try to be kind, and as honest as I can without being cruel, obnoxious, or rude. I try to be the best listener in the world and to be there whenever I can, and I show up exactly like that for myself, too.

People who have passed the "test" and do good by me, who inspire me and are free in their minds, enter and get a tattoo in my heart that comes with an unlimited credit card to my "energy account." I love them completely and unconditionally, even if we don't always agree on everything.

Of course, we never know what life brings to us, but as long as I stay loyal to myself and don't fool around, don't play with power or don't lie, I live well and the people in my life, too.

I meditate and express gratitude and love to God. I know the commitment that I have towards myself, and I will always try my best. So far, 16 years into my marriage, life is looking good. A clean, healthy, honest, faithful robust slate. Despite the wobbles, ups, and downs. What more can I do?

Sure, some rebellious voices in my head are still there, slightly different, weaker, gentler, and all in all harmless in comparison to the power of wisdom and love. But I am grateful that they never went away because they are a part of me. I got much better in letting only the loving voices have their say. The other ones, like the one that seduces, the one that punishes or the one that feels sad and helpless, have moved out. Now there's myself and me. We talk to each other like an old, married couple, with a smile, even when there is self-criticism.

I am far from perfect, but I'll get over that fact many times a day, and it's great. Despite my imperfections, I know that I am a person with a good heart, and I deserve happiness and a fantastic career because I work hard and put all my love and heart-blood in what I do like I did with this book for you, beloved reader.

Now I know a lot better, who I am, and how much love and devotion I can put into everything I do, into my friendships, and my family.

Life is full of the most fascinating smaller, or bigger mysteries, and the answer to them is most of the time right in front of us. If something makes me unhappy, like that audition that I bombed, I don't kill myself. Not the right people, not the right time, not the right place. But the right time, the right people and the right place are out there, too, all the time, continually passing right by our noses on invisible conveyor belts.

If we are not willing to sharpen our awareness for those blessings, we will have to make do with "what falls off the back of a delivery truck."

To end this autobiographical part, I want to conclude in the way I started: with the question of "How did I get to the point to love all food again, including former trigger foods like chocolate-mousse, croissants, ice-cream, pizza, and cookies?"

It was one of many choices that I made right there and then after the moment when I cried, seeing the woman with the croissant. Living now while embracing my past and the little confused girl I used to be, it started with a piece of pizza and real friends. The next day I had a whole-some healthy, homemade soup. The next slice of pizza tasted even better.

I made friends with those former "bad" junk-foods. I learned to enjoy them as treats while I shop for mainly whole foods and organic produce to use for my home cooking, which I do a lot. If the urge is gone to stuff yourself because your stomach muscles and digestion are back in shape and the hole in your soul is gone, you can eat less and feel full quickly. It feels much better than being stuffed because it is a feeling of satisfaction.

I don't have a scale at home. I don't need one. I don't want one. This thing is so triggering - no thanks. If you give your body what it needs in a balance, you are naturally slim. Since experiencing this with my own body, and understanding the principle of a healthy balance, not in WEIGHT-LOSS-AT-ALL-COST-terms that INCLUDES all yummy and happy food, eating is a pure pleasure again. Thanks to my choices and the blissful grace of the Universe, it's surprisingly easy.

Laying the right groundwork is of the essence: to get yourself to a point where you have sorted out your head and these old sentences and beliefs about yourself that made you feel horrible. Then there is space again for the dialogue with our body. It tells us everything.

We need to be happy.

The fuel you put in your body to FUNCTION is VITAL for your mental and physical health. Without a balanced diet, you won't have a single iota of a chance to develop a balanced mindset, and therefore a balance in your life. That means the body's shape is not the reason for your happiness; it is the result.

Whatever is out there to make you happy: go, get it. If you were crazy enough to try out an eating disorder, you are crazy enough to get the most amazing things, too. Choose amazingness. You are loved and worthy. <3

EPILOGUE

~ A Play, the Book, and a Song ~

The process of wanting to share my personal story started when I met the first person that opened up about her eating disorder.

It was mind-blowing to me how much of an impact my insights could have on someone else's life. Before meeting the first person who was actively suffering from this, it had never crossed my mind to share anything of my ED past on a larger scale - let alone "tainting" my image and branding as a filmmaker and actor! I once had tried so desperately to hide it from everyone.

So I began to openly mention my eating disorder past, when thoughts, that related to it, would pop up in my mind. The equation was what I expected: the more I talked about it, the more people confided in me, that they struggled with an eating disorder. Some were so desperate because of their unresolved eating disorder, that it kept me restless.

At a certain point in my life, I got the chance to move to New York. There, besides following my dream to be an actress, the desire to utilize what I learned about my eating disorder for others became an acute urgency.

Deep down, I knew that I had been holding myself back a little ever since my recovery. I felt concerned about getting lost in the world of glitz before I had accomplished specific personal goals, that I wanted to reach. Goals that were more significant to me than money or that my face is all over magazines. Regarding my career and becoming an actress and filmmaker, I also knew that I had to do something about bulimia. I made the connection: I wanted to share. But how?

I thought, "Please, dear Universe: can you hear me? I want to HELP and share my strength with people who are as sad and hopeless like I was! I want to help others to regain their full potential and joy of life, and I want them to know that they can be free and happy again and that it is NEVER too late to come back from this!"

The first answer came a day later in the shape of an audition invite in New York. It was for a play. When I read the description of the character and my lines, I was stunned – the play was about eating disorders. Do you think that this was a COINCIDENCE?! I most certainly did not.

The director and the writers wanted personal statements regarding the subject matter. I wrote a long e-mail to them, letting them know about me and my ED past. Check!

The audition was a few days later, and I had to prepare a monologue from the play. The day came, and I arrived in Brooklyn. I found the address, and entered this vast, industrial studio space where these fantastic looking, charismatic women greeted me. I performed the monologue, and every word came straight from the bottom of my heart. I had not forgotten anything about the voice of the illness. I had only stored it somewhere far deeper, hidden in the treasure chest of my heart.

When I finished, the women had tears in their eyes. It was almost chilling, how fast my wish to get active had materialized. As I walked to the subway, calling my hubby to let him know that the audition went GREAT and that I wanted to work with these lovely people, I had another call come in. They were offering me the part. Of course, I said yes.

When I received the full script, I found out that the actresses had written it themselves, based on their own stories. It was a moving experience for me to read the play with the actual faces attached to it.

Grateful and excited, I started digging my teeth deeply into the script and my character. Being allowed to dive into personal lives, getting to know the writers, and THEIR story so well was a real honor.

But as I studied the play, I had one big question in the end: what was their actual message? I read it again and again and wondered why there wasn't a glimpse of hope in the play, not to mention real recovery like I had experienced. Wasn't this the main piece of all? I mean, it's okay if the main message was to warn. But leaving out the magic ingredient that has a healing effect in itself, bugged me quite a bit.

I was eagerly looking forward to the next rehearsal so I could ask questions about the motive behind not offering this (at least in my eyes) missing piece. I understood that the play, despite the absence of hope, already had its profound value. As soon as you portray the subject authentically, people, and if it is only one person, are going to want to talk about it, and maybe someone even comes out of the closet. Every time in my life, when I spoke up about it, someone else did, too.

When there was a break, we sat together and talked. The opportunity to raise my question had come, and I just threw it out there and asked if it was on purpose to hold back with hopeful advice. The reply was: "Well, IS there a solution? IS there hope? Even if you stop doing it, WILL there be something good in the end, a happy end? Not really - right."

I looked in their faces and felt a deep, sad, collective sigh. I realized that everyone in the room was still raw, sliced open, and bleeding because of their eating disorders. Something inside me passionately made me stand up. I said: "Excuse me, ladies… but OF COURSE! Of course, there can be a good ending! It IS possible!"

I told my story in a short version that kept them almost in disbelief. There was this one particular actress, who dug her heels in and didn't want to believe me that I was enjoying food again. She interjected that I couldn't possibly be carefree if I really ever had "bulimia for real." She probably assumed that my toned and slender physique couldn't be possible without cheating a bit here and there.

However, after a long and heated discussion, everyone agreed that my request for hope might be a good idea.

When I left that night, I drove home with one of the actresses by train. She asked me about my roots, and I told her about Germany. She wanted to know more details, for example about the eating disorder awareness in Germany, and if the medical and therapeutic help was excellent.

I shrugged and replied that I didn't have a clue. She looked at me with HUGE eyes and said: but where did you go to therapy? I answered that I never had any sort of treatment. She asked, surprised: "But I thought, I mean, I understood, that you had a complete recovery?!" I answered: "Yes."

I was slightly confused about her logic, and I didn't put one and one together at first. Was a story like mine THAT unheard of and unbelievable? We smiled for a second in each other's eyes while the door opened and I had to get off the train.

We hugged. I could see in her facial expression that she was still confused, but I also picked up on something else: like at the Olympic Games, when they bring the fire from place to place, she had taken my flame. She had seen the truth in my eyes.

The ride home in the train that should get me to 51st Street where we lived at the time gave me a minute to realize: So, all these wonderful strong women who had written such a powerful play and were such compelling artists, yet they were all still sick, still trapped in various layers of their eating disorders. And, oh my God! Their reply to my suggestion has given me the answer of what I needed to do.

My way to help people (even if it is only one person), would be to spread the word that it IS possible to let go of this disease COMPLETELY - that loving food and eating again without thinking in bad or good foods was REAL.

I knew that night that my personal experience and the thousands of lessons learned needed to get out there. I researched support groups to spread the word about my healing and my message of hope, mouth to mouth.

Support group meetings, however, didn't work out. The only way to have uplifting conversations with sufferers was when I asked them if they wanted to meet up AFTER the tightly structured meetings, where people were only talking briefly about themselves. They were also mainly talking about their problems, sadness, and frustrations, and not really about their positive discoveries along the way. Please do not misunderstand me, these types of meetings are a GREAT step, but in my personal opinion, there was simply no space for people like me who could contribute greatly to someone's recovery journey.

The mere fact, that I was supposed to say, "Hi, my name is Annie, and I am a Bulimic" felt like a lie, and also like the opposite of my intention.

It was not helpful to the group dynamic, that I couldn't abide by the code. When I introduced myself as a fully recovered ex-bulimic, I was corrected and advised that we needed to stick to the rules. According to the rule book, addicts would always remain addicts, and the only distinction would be the length of their sobriety. This concept simply wasn't resonating with my own genuine story. I had left this part of my life entirely behind me.

Wasn't sobriety based on abstinence? How could I define myself as being sober, if I was eating everything and loving it, again? Or were they relating this to not bingeing and purging? Bingeing and purging were in no way a risk, danger, or temptation anymore. There was another conceptual factor, that didn't work for me in the support group setting: solutions were just read out loud from a book but not digested together, i.e., talked about in-depth. As beneficial, as this step could be, it was the wrong arena to open an unscripted conversation about input from others to heal.

I began to invite the people from the support group to tea right after the meeting, and most of them CAME. I was thrilled. I just wanted to listen and ask questions that would lead my new friends to a positive self-discovery. It was amazing! People go excited and hopeful. We laughed, cried and had a very inspirational vibe going. More people would join. Had I found the way to share my recovery gifts?

At first, this seemed like the perfect set-up, but soon after, more and more calls and texts would pour in after those after-meeting-tea's that started to get longer and longer. I felt exhausted and unable to serve as much as I wanted to.

I so desperately wanted to help. I would have loved to cut myself in a thousand pieces and put myself in all of the lovely, amazing people's pockets to be them when they needed me. But I started to fall behind in regards to showing up for myself. Not exhausting myself while my acting career moved in the background, had become a challenge.

If I couldn't make it to a meeting, I felt dreadful, as if I was letting everyone down. I felt helpless regarding the demand of help needed. The one-on-one situation I had set up out of desperate attempt to do something was not going to work for me. It wasn't the career and life-path that I could walk in this way. There was a REASON why I had decided not to study to become a healthcare professional. I was an artist and not doing what I owed to myself.

I started to record a few YouTube videos but realized that I had almost the same problem that I had with meeting people in real life because more and more people started to contact me, and it got too overwhelming, way too quick.

While my thoughts revolved more and more around how much need and confusion there was while I so badly wanted to make a positive change, my life-energy poured right out of me again, and that could not be a suitable path, either.

As always, I sat down to quieten my mind and pondered, trying to define the issue at hand. Out of the blue, a vision of a book popped up. A book!

Right, a book could be some sort of "cutting myself in a thousand pieces." I could take the time to say what I had to say. I could do this without moving my acting, dancing, singing, directing, painting, writing in the background. The book was IT. Instead of spreading my focus all over the show, I promised myself and to the Universe, that I would do this properly. The next morning, I sat down and wrote the first page.

And now, many years later, I am sitting in Los Angeles in my local coffee shop after my large latte and croissant, surrounded by laughter, great smells, music, and lovely people, and I am finally closing the last chapter. This book, my life, my most sacred conclusions, and secrets are between a few hundred pages that I have dedicated to you and your healing.

Throughout this long writing journey, until today, until now, it amazed me over and over, what magnificent creators we human beings are. How happy I am that I have started and finished this book. What is a good start for you to begin the work on your happy end?

It is an excellent start to envision the person you want to be. Bring some real good humor to the table.

Look for angels close to you, who are great listeners and non-judgmental. That's a significant perk that comes with therapy, as I would find out a little later down the line when I did my undercover research for Book 3, taking place at the treatment centers in New York. People (usually!) don't judge you in a treatment center. In my eyes, this is, as you know now, one of the key elements regarding healing from eating disorders.

If we stop judging each other, we can also stop judging ourselves. Judging is, like nailing someone down onto something. It doesn't work. We are in permanent flow, development, and flux. We are like metal. If we are around the fire, we get soft, and if we are in the cold, we get stiff.

What can you do when you are in the wrong environment? RUN. If you have "friends" like those "energy-vampires,'" RUN.

If you have a toxic partner: RUN, it's a bit more problematic with the parents, but instead of running, there are other options.

The promise that once you are old enough, you can create your own, perfect, healthy, and happy world, and life, no matter what has happened to you in the past, is real. And being old enough is not a question of age. Some mature women and men are still battling with their hidden trauma of abuse from when they were a child, and they are stuck right there.

And as you might know best: everyone has a hidden story. The one seemingly big problem that you might be experiencing right now is likely, as it was in my case, a sum of a lot of smaller issues. Breaking them down and releasing them bit by bit is what we will explore in the next volume of the book, and I hope you will find answers, inspiration, and, most importantly, your innate self-love.

You are a blessed being, because you are alive, and you are worthy of only the best. Nature intended you to be happy and fulfilled, and you deserve all of the miracles and joy that you could experience.

Yes, it's true. You know why? Because happy people take better care of this planet and all the living beings in it. It's not your fault - that terrible, mind-boggling disease that you caught. It HAPPENED to you. None of what happened to you is your fault, and you are not alone, either. You just didn't know better at the time, and you just got stuck. But you CAN get out.

Reach out and open up. Become that expert of yourself. Choose the best for yourself, for your happiness, for your well-being, for your recovery.

Choose the best of all of your dreams, so that they can come true and do not put a cap on them. Stay open-minded, and your story remains open-ended. It is possible, and you can do it. SELF-ADVOCAY, BABY!!

Allow as much love as possible back into your life and onto your plate, and into your mouth, and please, start by giving all of the love you have on offer to yourself first.

You were born to thrive beyond measure. And when you succeed, you serve others.

Before I release you now from accompanying me along the winding road of my personal life story, I want to part with a song that I wrote - I dedicated it to YOU <3

It's Your Time

Starting with the day of birth

When we arrive on this planet called earth

We were thrown into a spiral of action and reaction

To some better or worse attraction

We are looking for explanations

Try to understand our races, colors nations

But in all our searching we sometimes forget to stop

For a little while to breathe and smile

It's your time your golden moment in time

On your endless journey, right through silent clocks

Dance with fire on the sea, your solo, In your heart in your eyes, in your smile…

And now we run from date to date Always worried about being late

What are we running from, or better, running to?

Most of the time from our own God-given beauty,

Distract ourselves and getting blinded

By the veils of limits and borders

This experience is magic

Why can't we see it all the time and realize

It's our time our golden moment in time

On our endless journey right through silent clocks

Dance with fire on the sea, our solo, In our hearts in our eyes, in our smiles

Shines a light so strong and endless,

It is stronger than death and pain

We can send it once across the universe

If we just let peace and love reign

We can save lives we can lift up

And stop people's cry just with our love

Hold God's hand and trust in his guiding voice

And realize that everything

Is really our own choice.

So take the best – and realize

It's your time, your golden moment in time

On your endless journey, a dance of love

Through all silent clocks

In your heart, in your eyes, in your smile,

I see Eternity.

Beloved reader and friend, your life is waiting for you with so much real, happiness and fun and so many wonders, waiting only for you and no one else. You are worthy. You are beautiful. You are the expression of love, poetry in motion, you are made of the stars and meant to soar. You can rise above anything if you apply your mind, heart, and devotion to it, and most importantly, your self-forgiveness and self-love. It's your time - your time to be happy and free. Follow your bliss, my fellow traveler.

Be unstoppable. Don't settle for anything less than joy, so follow the trumpet calls that accompany your path as it lights up under your feet. I want to see you dance your solo - because no one else can do it. You are needed in this world and wanted. You matter to me, and I believe in you, no matter what. Now, get those wings and fly.

I LOVE YOU.

Printed in Great Britain
by Amazon